DATE DUE

DEMCO 38-296

RICHARD M.
NIXON

RICHARD M. NIXON

HERÓN MÁRQUEZ

LERNER PUBLICATIONS COMPANY / MINNEAPOLIS

To Baby 3M, Baby Chardonnay, Baby Dave, and Sparky.
We'll miss you.

Lerner Publications Company
A division of Lerner Publishing Group
241 First Avenue North
Minneapolis, MN 55401 U.S.A.

Website address: www.lernerbooks.com

Library of Congress Cataloging-in-Publication Data

Márquez, Herón
    Richard Nixon / by Herón Márquez.
        p.   cm. — (Presidential leaders)
    Includes bibliographical references and index.
    ISBN: 0–8225–0098–1 (lib. bdg. : alk. paper)
    1. Nixon, Richard M. (Richard Milhous), 1913–1994—Juvenile literature. 2. Presidents—United States—Biography—Juvenile literature. [1. Nixon, Richard M. (Richard Milhous), 1913–1994. Presidents.] I. Title. II. Series
    E856 .M264 2003
    973.924'092—dc21   2001007209

Manufactured in the United States of America
1 2 3 4 5 6 – JR – 08 07 06 05 04 03

CONTENTS

⸻ ✧ ⸻

Richard Nixon's career was marked by great achievement, politically fatal poor judgment, and questionable ethics.

INTRODUCTION

There were good legal grounds for a challenge. . . . My heart told me to do it, my head said no.

—Richard Nixon, referring to
the 1960 presidential election results

The 2000 presidential election between George W. Bush and Al Gore was probably the most controversial race for the White House in history. Vote-counting problems surfaced in several states, including Florida. Gore challenged the Florida results in state and federal courts, eventually reaching the United States Supreme Court. The court battles kept the country waiting to learn who would be president.

A lot of pressure was put on Gore to give up his court fights because they were delaying the naming of a president. Gore refused, and the turmoil continued for more than a month after the November 7 election. Finally, on December 12, the Supreme Court declared Bush the official winner. Media and political commentators immediately started making comparisons to the 1960 presidential race between Richard Milhous Nixon and John Fitzgerald Kennedy.

*With his wife, Pat, at his side, Nixon conceded the 1960
presidential election as a gesture of goodwill and political savvy,
hoping to secure his future in public life.*

Back then, Nixon had accepted a controversial defeat to
John F. Kennedy in order to spare the country a messy
legal fight. Nixon had lost to Kennedy by about 113,000
votes, one of the closest races in U.S. history. Many
Republicans believed that Kennedy and the Democrats had
stolen the election from Nixon by having illegal votes cast
in Illinois and Texas, two key states because of the large
number of votes they represented. Some historians believe
Nixon had a good case and that the election may have
been tainted. "Despite the intensity of the campaign and
the narrow outcome, he accepted the results with grace
and without rancor," Kennedy's brother Senator Edward
M. Kennedy said years later in praise of Nixon's decision.

Nixon decided that a legal challenge would probably have
taken almost a year, leaving the United States without an
elected president during that time. Nixon also knew that if he
were to contest the election he would be labeled a sore loser,

possibly hurting his chance for future political office. Above all else, Richard Nixon wanted someday to be president.

Nixon accepted his defeat graciously. In the noblest act of his life as a politician, Nixon congratulated Kennedy on his victory and returned quietly to his home in California. Two years later, Nixon ran for governor of California, even though he really didn't want the job.

When he lost the governor's race, he told the media that he was quitting politics, but Nixon remained one of the best-known politicians in the world. He continued to campaign for Republicans around the country, so by 1968 he was in a position to reconsider his decision to quit politics. He accepted the Republican nomination for president to run against Minnesota's Hubert H. Humphrey, the Democratic nominee.

──────────── ✧

Vice President Nixon (right) congratulates president-elect John F. Kennedy (left) on his victory just days after the November 1960 election.

In November 1968, Nixon was elected president of the United States. He was finally the most powerful man in the world, perhaps partly because he had done an honorable thing in 1960. Unfortunately, it was not a lesson Nixon was to learn well. Within months of being elected, he was involved in a series of illegal acts—wiretapping aides, political opponents, and journalists.

Within a few years after being reelected, Nixon became involved in one of the most infamous political capers in history: the break-in at the Watergate office complex in Washington, D.C. The incident and cover-up eventually led to an impeachment inquiry and cost Nixon what he treasured most, the presidency.

Richard Nixon takes the oath of office on January 20, 1969, becoming the thirty-seventh president of the United States.

IMPEACHMENT

The impeachment process is a means of removing a civilian government official—either elected or appointed—from office for serious misconduct. The process is spelled out in the U.S. Constitution. The officeholder must first be charged with doing something illegal or improper, which the Constitution states can be charges of treason, bribery, or other high crimes and misdemeanors. The process involves the House of Representatives (the House), the Senate, and the U.S. Supreme Court.

The process begins with the House Judiciary Committee debating whether to start an impeachment inquiry against the accused—the president, for example. The committee then seeks a resolution from the entire House of Representatives to conduct the inquiry. A majority vote is required from the House to pass the resolution. Once this is done, the committee holds the inquiry, sometimes in a public hearing. Articles of impeachment are then prepared and approved by a majority vote of the committee. The full House then debates and votes on each article of impeachment. If one or more articles are approved, then the president is considered impeached. Nixon, for example, was impeached on three charges: abuse of power, obstruction of justice, and impeding impeachment by defying the committee's subpoenas.

The process then moves to the Senate, which holds an impeachment trial. The senators serve as the jury, and the chief justice of the Supreme Court presides at the trial. As at any trial, evidence is presented by both sides. At the end of the trial, the Senate votes on whether to remove the president from office. A two-thirds majority of the senators present is required to remove an officeholder. If the president is removed, then the vice president becomes the president, as outlined in the Constitution.

CHAPTER ONE

LIFE AND DEATH

What starts the process really are laughs and slights and snubs when you are a kid . . . if your anger is deep enough and strong enough you learn that you can change those attitudes.

—Richard Nixon, talking about changing the judgmental attitudes of others

As president of the United States, Richard Nixon lived in Washington, D.C., in the White House, the ultimate symbol of power and prestige with its large white columns and impressive lawns. But the future president began life on January 9, 1913, in a small, humble house his father, Francis, had built in a lemon grove in Yorba Linda, California.

Francis Nixon, called Frank, was born on a farm in Elk Township, Ohio, on December 3, 1878. The elder Nixon was known as a strict disciplinarian who also had a bad temper. "My father was a scrappy, belligerent fighter, with a quick, wide-ranging raw intellect," Richard Nixon recalled as an adult. "He left me with a respect for learning and hard work, and the will to keep fighting no matter what the odds. . . . My father had an Irish quickness both to anger and to mirth. It was his temper that impressed me most as a small child."

Francis "Frank" Nixon

——————— ◇ ———————

Frank worked at a variety of jobs as a young man. He had worked as a carpenter, hauled logs to a sawmill, and managed a potato farm. One of Frank Nixon's jobs was working as a streetcar motorman, taking tickets from passengers while standing on a platform outside the vehicle. In 1906 he suffered frostbite on his feet because his cubicle was unheated. He protested to the company but that got no results, so he organized a protest by the other motormen. Then he got the Ohio State Legislature to pass a bill requiring heated and enclosed areas for motormen.

Shortly thereafter he moved to the warmer climate of California, where he met Hannah Milhous in 1908. Hannah was born on March 7, 1885, in Butlerville, Indiana, one of nine children. The family all believed deeply in the Quaker religion. In 1897 the Milhous family moved to California, settling in Whittier, which had a large Quaker population. There she met Frank Nixon. After a courtship of only four months, the couple married. The Milhous family loaned the couple money to start the Yorba Linda lemon farm.

Richard Nixon was the second of five boys born to Francis and Hannah Nixon. The oldest son, Harold, was born in 1909 and died from tuberculosis in 1933, when he was twenty-four. A third son, Francis Donald, was born in 1914. Arthur, who was born in 1918, fell ill and died unexpectedly of tuberculosis in 1925 when Richard was twelve. The fifth boy, Edward, was born in 1930.

The boys, except for Francis who was named after his father, were all named after some of the early kings of England. Richard was named after King Richard the Lionhearted, who was king of England from 1189 to 1199.

Richard's first memory is of riding with his mother, his brother Donald, and a neighbor girl in a horse-drawn carriage at the age of three. He slipped and fell when the buggy went around a turn too fast.

✧ —————————

A young Nixon (right) with his mother, Hannah, father, Francis, and brothers, Francis (center) and Harold (left) in 1917

Young Nixon (center with cap) *and his brothers playfully mug for the camera in the early 1920s.*

He chased after his mother, who was in the carriage trying to get the horses to stop. When she finally did, she took the boy to a doctor twenty-five miles away to have a large cut on his head stitched up. Richard Nixon said later that after the fall he always wore his hair straight back to cover the scar.

The Nixon family was not dirt poor, but it was not well off either. The lemon farm was not profitable, so the family grew its own food. The boys had to pitch in to help around the farm while Frank Nixon worked as a carpenter, building houses. The small house the family lived in had no heat and no indoor plumbing. The family had to use an outhouse in the backyard. The four boys shared a small upstairs bedroom. "It was crowded," Richard Nixon recalled. "But except for the occasional pillow fights, we got along famously."

Hannah's strong connection to the Quakers, also called the Society of Friends, remained throughout her life. Each Nixon family meal was started with a prayer, and young Richard recalled that his mother went into a closet each night to pray in private. She made sure her family was equally religious, requiring her sons to go to Quaker religious meetings four times on Sundays. Also, the whole family drove to nearby Los Angeles during the week to listen to evangelists (preachers) at the Trinity Methodist Church.

Frank Nixon was a strong Republican who supported the elections of Warren G. Harding and Calvin Coolidge for president. Richard Nixon recalls sitting at the dinner table while his father talked politics. His father's political passion caught the boy's attention, and it did not take long for the child's own interest in politics to surface.

A cousin, Merle West, recalls walking to school in 1920 when Warren Harding was running for president. Near the school, she saw her young cousin Dick, as Richard was called, standing on a tree stump telling people why they should vote for Harding.

✧ ——————

A young fan of politics, Nixon, age eight, followed his father's political ideas and supported Republican Warren G. Harding (left) for president in 1920.

Political articles and images like the one at right exposed the Teapot Dome scandal. After reading such articles, young Nixon decided he wanted to be a politician and do right by people.
—————————— ✦

At the age of nine, after Harding was elected, young Nixon read in the paper one day about the Teapot Dome scandal. Harding's interior secretary, Albert Fall, had secretly leased government oil fields at Teapot Dome, Wyoming, and Elk Hills, California, to friends of his. Congress was investigating the deal because Fall had received illegal payments from the oil men in return for leasing the public land.

Nixon's mother recalls that her son looked at her while reading about the scandal and said he was going to grow up to be a lawyer whom no one could bribe. By the time he reached the eighth grade, young Nixon wrote in an essay that he wanted to be a lawyer and a politician when he grew up so he could do some good for people.

The Nixon family moved to the nearby town of Whittier in 1922 because the lemon farm had failed. Whittier was a small town of only a few hundred people with no bars, no liquor stores, and no dance halls. Frank Nixon moved the family there after he bought a gas station on a highway outside of town. He had seen that cars, then called horseless carriages, were going to be a big part of the country's future, so he thought a gas station would do big business. He was right. Soon there was so much business pulling into the gas station that Frank added a grocery store, where the four brothers worked while growing up. The prize attraction at the Nixon store was Hannah's pies and cakes, especially her homemade angel food cake.

Frank Nixon expected hard work of all his boys, who were reminded constantly that it would take hard work to get anywhere in life. Nixon remembers that his father often told the boys, especially him, that they would have to work hard because they were not going to go very far on their looks.

When Richard got older, he was put in charge of buying the fresh fruit and vegetables from the farmer's market in Los Angeles. He recalls getting up at four o'clock in the morning so he could be at the market by five o'clock to buy the best produce. He then washed the fruit and vegetables, got them displayed, and got to school by eight o'clock.

This hard schedule did not prevent Richard from doing well in school. Hannah had taught her son to read before he entered school, and the boy worked hard and soon became one of the best students in the school. Even in first grade, he sat for hours by the fireplace reading such magazines as the *Saturday Evening Post,* the *Ladies' Home Journal,* and *National Geographic,* his favorite.

Throughout his academic life, Nixon was always one of the top two or three students in whatever school he attended. "He was one of those rare individuals," recalled his first teacher, Mary George. "He just never had to work for knowledge at all. He was told something and he never forgot. He was a very quiet, studious boy . . . a solemn child who rarely ever smiled or laughed."

Nixon also had a sensitive and artistic side as a boy. He was an accomplished musician on the piano, violin, saxophone, and clarinet. Although he outgrew his preschool dream of being a train engineer, Nixon maintained his love of music throughout his life. "I have often thought that if there had been a good rap group around in those days I might have chosen a career in music instead of politics," Nixon recalled about his childhood.

The death of his two brothers, especially Arthur in 1925, hit young Richard hard, and his mother believes it pushed him to become successful in life. Friends and relatives say he thought he could make up to his parents for the loss of Arthur, who had died at the age of seven. "I think it was Arthur's passing that first stirred within Richard a determination to help make up for our loss, by making us very proud of him," Hannah recalled. "Now his need to succeed became even stronger."

Nixon proved to be extremely successful in high school. Helped by an incredibly good memory, Nixon became a star member of the school debate team. He took part in school plays and was named one of the top students in California. He was a member of the school newspaper and played violin in the school orchestra. Nixon also tried his hand at politics for the first time when he ran for class president as a junior at Whittier High School. He lost.

Nixon longed to go to a famous Ivy League university on the East Coast. He came close when, upon graduating from high school in 1930, Harvard and Yale Universities invited him to apply for scholarships. The timing, however, was not good. The Great Depression (a period of economic hardship) had begun, so the Nixon family, like many others, did not have much money. Also, Nixon graduated just as his brother Harold was dying of tuberculosis. The family needed Nixon at home, so he had to decline Harvard and Yale and instead attend Whittier College.

Although disappointed, he continued to work hard. He became a good actor in school plays and a champion debater and was elected student body president in 1933. He also played on the college football team, although he admits he was not very good and would only get in at the end when the team was winning or losing by a lot.

While at Whittier, Nixon applied for membership in the prestigious Franklin Club. The group, made up of wealthy boys at the school, turned him down, perhaps because his family was not well off. Nixon then did something character-istic. In order to prove he was just as good as the privileged students, he joined a newly created competing club called the Orthogonians, for square-shooters—just or honest people.

Nixon shown as a member of the football team (left) *and the Orthogonians Club* (right) *at Whittier College*

The group, made up mainly of working-class boys, admitted only students working their way through school, like Nixon. The boys took pride in the fact that they didn't wear ties, ate spaghetti instead of steak, and wore short-sleeved shirts.

Despite the disappointment of not going to an Ivy League school and not getting into the Franklin Club, Nixon continued to work hard at Whittier and graduated number two in his class. Upon graduation he fulfilled part of his dream by going east to go to law school. Nixon applied for a scholarship and was accepted at Duke University Law School in North Carolina.

While at Duke, Nixon continued to outwork just about everybody who competed against him. He spent so much time studying, and was so serious all the time, that classmates called him Gloomy Gus. Once again, the hard work paid off as Nixon graduated third in his class. He was even elected president of the Duke Student Bar Association.

Nixon hoped to use his good academic standing to get a job with the Federal Bureau of Investigation (FBI) or with a prestigious East Coast law firm in New York. Once again he was frustrated in his efforts to become part of the East Coast establishment of money and power. The FBI turned him down because it did not have enough money to hire new agents, and his applications to East Coast law firms were rejected. With no better alternatives, he returned to Whittier. His mother helped him get a job at a local law firm, Wingert and Bewley.

Nixon handled mainly divorces and business-related cases. But small town law proved boring, so he looked for something more challenging to do. He joined community and business groups, hoping to make political contacts.

Nixon continued to act in community plays. During a 1938 audition for a play called *The Dark Tower,* Nixon met a beautiful redhead named Thelma Catherine Ryan. Her father had given her the nickname of Pat, and that was how she was commonly known. Like Nixon, Pat Ryan had worked her way through college. Among her jobs was being an extra in Hollywood movies. She became a teacher at Whittier High after graduation from the University of Southern California in 1937.

Nixon recalls that it was love at first sight when he met Pat. He recalls telling her, before they'd even had a first date, that he was going to marry her someday. It took him two years to convince her, but the couple was finally married on June 21,1940, about a year after World War II had broken out in Europe.

About this time, Nixon told a friend about his interest in politics and about how he thought he would be president of the United States one day. Those political ambitions were put on hold as World War II raged on. The Nixons were given a chance to move to Washington, D.C., where Richard Nixon got a job as a lawyer for the government's Office of Price Administration (OPA). The OPA's job was to monitor and control prices so the rate of inflation in the country could be managed during the war.

In the summer of 1942, eight months after the Japanese had bombed the U.S. naval base at Pearl Harbor, Hawaii, Nixon enlisted in the navy as a lieutenant commander. He was sent to the Solomon Islands in the South Pacific Ocean. While there Nixon helped to direct the transport and movement of soldiers. Thousands of miles from home, Nixon felt stranded even farther away from his political dreams.

CHAPTER TWO

FLUSH WITH SUCCESS

*My dad used to say when we were growing up,
he said, "You know, you boys"—speaking to
me particularly—"you boys have got to get out
and scratch. You're not going to get anywhere
on your good looks."*

—Richard Nixon

Although most of the world was at war, Nixon's life in the
South Pacific was relatively boring. The heat and humidity,
along with the isolation of being on a tropical island, made
the time drag. The only bright spots were the letters the men
got from their wives and sweethearts. Nixon was never actu-
ally in combat, so he passed the time teaching law courses to
some of his fellow sailors. They, in turn, taught Nixon a new
skill, playing poker. "The pressures of wartime, and the even
more oppressive monotony, made it an irresistible diversion,"
Nixon wrote about playing cards. "I found playing poker
instructive as well as entertaining and profitable."

*His keen wits and drive to win earned Nixon (right) the reputation of
a sly and adept poker player during his service in the U.S. Navy.*

———————————— ◇ ————————————

Throughout his life, Nixon was modest about his card-
playing abilities, but he took the game seriously. Those who
played with and against Nixon remember him being a
skilled player who made a good living playing poker. "He
won . . . more frequently than he lost and he sent home to
California a fair amount of money," said James Stewart, the
naval officer who taught Nixon how to play. "I have no
idea exactly how much, but my estimate was between
$6,000 and $7,000." In the early 1940s, that was a lot of
money, enough to buy a house, a car, and maybe even to
launch a political career.

The war ended in 1945. The next year, Nixon left the
military, and he and Pat also became parents. Patricia, always
called Tricia, was born on February 21, 1946. Soon after the
birth came a brief note from Herman Perry, a banker friend

in Whittier. Perry asked Nixon if he was interested in running for office against Congressman Jerry Voorhis in Whittier in 1946. Voorhis was everything that Richard Nixon was not. Voorhis was rich, a graduate of Yale University, a strong believer in government's involvement in people's lives, and someone who had been in Congress for more than ten years.

Voorhis, first elected in 1936, was not well liked by Republican businessmen in Whittier. Perry told Nixon he was confident that Nixon was smart enough and tough enough to take on Voorhis and win. Almost everyone else thought Voorhis was unbeatable, however, and few people gave Nixon a chance. But Nixon proved people wrong.

With the same determination he had used in school, Nixon simply outworked and outthought everyone. Nixon studied Voorhis's record until he knew it better than Voorhis. Nixon then pointed out how good he would be (how he worked for everything in his life) and how bad his opponent was for the district. He painted Voorhis as a rich boy who didn't know how government worked.

—————————— ✧

At age thirty-three, Nixon ran for a seat in the U.S. House of Representatives.

Nixon also looked around at what scared people the most, then used that to his advantage. After the war, the biggest fear was Communism, a political system in which the government controls the means of production and citizens have few liberties. After World War II, the Union of Soviet Socialist Republics (USSR) was the biggest Communist government in the world, and fear of Soviet expansion increased as the Soviet Union became more and more powerful.

Nixon implied, but never quite said, that Voorhis was a Communist. At that time, being labeled a Communist was about as bad a name as anyone could be called in public. The win-at-any-cost attitude worked. During a series of debates, Nixon outfoxed his opponent, pointing out that Voorhis had introduced no significant bills during his time in Congress. He also pointed out that Communist groups supported Voorhis.

At age thirty-three, Nixon was elected to Congress with almost 60 percent of the vote, getting 65,586 votes to Voorhis's 49,994. Nixon had learned some valuable lessons: tapping into people's fears, working hard, and at times stretching the truth could lead to political success. "All the stops were pulled out and Mr. Nixon beat me," Voorhis recalled years later. "He was a good debater, he was a clever debater. I wouldn't deny that at all, but I still feel that there were a good many below-the-belt blows struck in the campaign."

For Nixon the second part of his dream was finally accomplished. Not only had he become a lawyer, he was also a politician. To Nixon the ends he achieved justified the means he had used to be elected. Nixon knew that

Jerry Voorhis wasn't a Communist, but he so wanted to win that he was willing to run what he termed an aggressive campaign against him. "Since Voorhis was the front-runner and I a newcomer, I ran an especially vigorous campaign," Nixon recalled. "I challenged his judgment and his voting record. . . . If some of my rhetoric seems overstated now, it was nonetheless in keeping with the approach that seasoned Republican politicians were using that year." Attacking Communism is one of the things for which Nixon is most remembered.

As a member of the U.S. House of Representatives, Nixon's first appointment was to the House Education and Labor Committee. He was joined on this committee by freshman congressman John Fitzgerald Kennedy (JFK) from Massachusetts. The meeting was the start of a rivalry between the two men. Kennedy—rich, good looking, and with a natural confidence—was almost the complete opposite of Nixon. What the two men had in common was a great ambition to be president. Over the years, Nixon became well known as a hardworking politician. Kennedy was seen as less serious, someone more interested in having fun than working hard.

Nixon made his first visit to the White House on February 18, 1947, when he and three other congressmen attended a private reception with President Harry Truman. The visit impressed Nixon, who at this time was as happy as he had ever been in his life. The joy increased when, on July 5, 1948, the Nixons' second daughter, Julie, was born.

Nixon's rise to prominence began about a month after Julie's birth, when he became involved in a famous spy case. After entering Congress, Nixon had also been given a position on the House Committee on Un-American Activities. Just after World War II, the Cold War had started between the United States and the Soviet Union. The Cold War did not involve actual fighting. Instead, the United States and the Soviet Union were competing with one another for influence around the world.

The committee was created because the U.S. government was worried about Communist influences within the United States. Nixon and the committee were given the job of finding Communists or Soviet sympathizers in the United States. These people, many of them U.S. citizens, were called Reds because the Soviet Union's flag was red.

During the war, Nixon had supported the Soviet Union because the Soviets were fighting Germany, a U.S. enemy. But when he saw how the Soviets had taken over Eastern Europe after the war, Nixon changed his mind and became anti-Communist.

Nixon did a good job going after suspected Communists— too good a job in the eyes of many critics. They complained that Nixon was too aggressive in going after people, destroying their lives on little evidence. For example, Nixon took on a group of ten Hollywood movie scriptwriters. They were called to testify before the committee about what they knew about Communists working in the movie industry.

The group, called the Hollywood Ten, refused to testify. They did not think that the committee was fair, because most of the members were avid anti-Communists. The group also thought the committee was violating their First Amendment rights to free speech and free association. In a fiery speech, Nixon demanded that the group be held in contempt of Congress, and they were jailed for a time.

Once the group got out of jail, they were blacklisted and not hired to work on serious movies again in Hollywood.

Nixon's most famous case involved a well-known politician named Alger Hiss. A lawyer in Baltimore, Maryland, Hiss had been a high State Department official and a friend of President Franklin Delano Roosevelt. Hiss, who had helped found the United Nations, was accused of being a spy and passing government secrets to the Soviet Union. No one believed the accusation at first. But Nixon was convinced that Hiss was a spy, so he insisted that the committee hold hearings to prove it. The move was a big gamble. If Nixon was wrong, or if he could not prove his accusations, his career as a politician would probably be over. He would never get to be president, or even senator.

Hour after hour and day after day, Nixon threw himself into the Hiss case. His wife, Pat, became concerned that he was being consumed by it. Nixon grew even more intense as

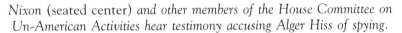

Nixon (seated center) *and other members of the House Committee on Un-American Activities hear testimony accusing Alger Hiss of spying.*

A *determined Congressman Nixon* (right) *examines microfilm with Chief Investigator Robert Stripling* (left) *during the Alger Hiss hearings.*

⸻ ✧ ⸻

it took longer and longer to prove Hiss was betraying the government. Newscasters and critics began wondering if Nixon, not Hiss, was the one lying. But Nixon remained convinced that he was right. "Mother, I think Hiss is lying," he wrote to Hannah Nixon during the investigation. "Until I know the truth, I've got to stick it out."

The big break in the case came when an editor at *Time* magazine named Whittaker Chambers said he could prove that Hiss was a spy. Chambers had been a Communist and a spy for the Soviets. He declared that he and Hiss were working together, and he could prove it. He said that secret papers given to him by Hiss were hidden in a pumpkin on Chambers's farm in Maryland. Police raided the farm on December 2, 1948, and found microfilm of stolen documents Hiss allegedly had taken from the U.S. State Department. The documents, known as the "Pumpkin Papers," were enough to prove Hiss had been lying. Nixon had been proved right.

Nixon found out about the discovery while he was on vacation, cruising the Caribbean Sea with his family. He got a telegram from Robert Stripling, the committee's chief investigator, asking Nixon to return to Washington. Nixon was picked up from the ship by a U.S. Coast Guard plane. Hiss was finally convicted in 1950, after two trials. He was sentenced to five years in prison for perjury, or lying under oath to Congress.

The publicity from the Hiss case made Nixon one of the most famous and most hated politicians in the country. To many Republicans and conservatives, the Hiss case proved that Nixon was a great anti-Communist, and to them this meant a great defender of the United States. But most Democrats and liberals disliked Nixon because they thought he was too harsh and too unprincipled in trying to demonstrate a "Red Scare."

Nixon's suspicions of Hiss were publically verified when a federal grand jury found Hiss guilty of two counts of perjury in 1950.

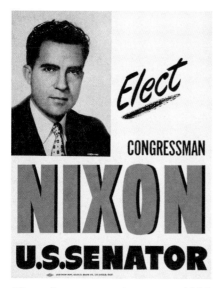

Nixon Senate campaign poster, 1950
——————— ✧ ———————

Nixon didn't care if people hated him. He had won, and he quickly looked for ways to take advantage of his new fame. He decided to pursue an even more powerful job—U.S. senator. His opponent would be Helen Gahagan Douglas, a former actress who was running for senator from California. At the time, Nixon was only thirty-five years old.

Although Nixon did not openly accuse Douglas of being a Communist, he did the next best thing. People who were not Communists but who were sympathetic to Communist causes were called "pinks" or "pinkos." So Nixon started calling Douglas, who was a liberal and not worried about any Communist threat, a "pink lady." Nixon sent out campaign flyers against Douglas on pink paper. He said Douglas was pink right down to her underwear. Also, just before the election, Nixon supporters made about 500,000 calls to voters in California asking if they knew that Douglas was a Communist.

Douglas, married to movie actor Melvyn Douglas, tried to fight back but without success. She called Nixon a peewee who was trying to scare people into voting for him. Douglas did succeed at pinning a nickname on Nixon that was to haunt him until he died. Because of all the dirty tricks he pulled, Douglas called Nixon "Tricky Dick." Still, Nixon won by more than 700,000 votes.

With the Senate victory, Nixon moved toward his ultimate goal of becoming president. The next step along that path was provided by a World War II hero, General Dwight D. Eisenhower. The retired general, known as Ike, was running for president as a Republican in 1952. He selected Nixon to be his vice presidential candidate. Ike liked the fact that Nixon was young, aggressive, and came from California, an important state politically because of its large population.

CHAPTER THREE

A SERIOUS GAME OF CHECKERS

*I have a theory... that the best and only answer
to a smear or to an honest misunderstanding of
the facts is to tell the truth.*
—Richard Nixon

Just as Nixon began to experience the joys of being the vice presidential candidate, he almost lost the job. Just after Eisenhower chose Nixon to be his running mate, a political scandal broke out around him. In September 1952, the *New York Post* newspaper reported that wealthy friends of Nixon had set up a secret fund of $18,000 for Nixon's personal use, which made it seem as if he were accepting bribes.

Nixon learned about the money while he and Eisenhower were campaigning around the country on separate trains. "The charge was false, but it hit like a bombshell on our train and a nuclear explosion on Eisenhower's," Nixon later wrote.

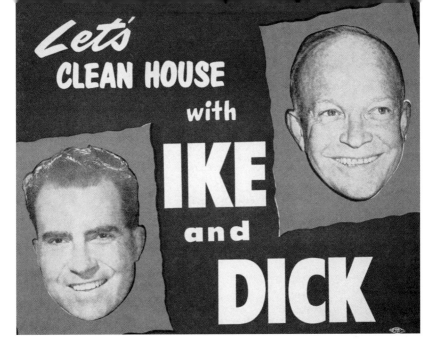

Eisenhower and Nixon, promising to "clean house," ran against the supposed corruption of the Truman administration.

The charge was especially troubling because Eisenhower and Nixon were campaigning against the scandals of President Harry Truman's administration. The scandals included allegations of influence peddling, tax fraud at the Internal Revenue Service (IRS), kickbacks, and the acceptance of improper gifts.

The story caused a huge outcry around the country. People began demanding that Eisenhower drop Nixon from the presidential ticket because he was an embarrassment. Nixon and the people who ran the secret fund tried to stop the controversy by saying the money was not for Nixon's personal use. They said it was supposed to be used strictly for political expenses, such as office supplies, campaign ads, and travel-related costs. Newspapers and important political observers demanded that Nixon resign. Among the papers that requested Nixon's resignation was the *New York Times,* a newspaper that Nixon always hated because he thought it was too liberal.

Eisenhower told Nixon that the only way he could salvage his place on the ticket was to come clean, to make a speech to the nation explaining the whole situation. The only way he could do that, Eisenhower said, was to show the public all of his finances. Nixon would not only have to explain the secret fund but also tell the public about all the things that he owned and the debts that he owed.

Nixon took the unusual step of using television to give the address. Television technology was only a few years old, but Nixon and the Republicans thought it was worth spending $75,000 to buy the television time needed to broadcast the speech. It was the first time that TV would be used for such a political purpose. On September 23, 1952, Nixon spoke before a television audience of 58 million people.

"My fellow Americans," Nixon began, "I come before you tonight as a candidate for the vice presidency and as a man whose honesty and integrity has been questioned. . . . And so now . . . I am going at this time to give this television and radio audience, a complete financial history, everything I've earned, everything I've spent, everything I owe."

Nixon mentioned that the Nixon family owned a house in Washington, D.C., which cost $41,000, and on which he owed $20,000; a house in Whittier that cost $13,000 and on which he still owed $3,000. He also mentioned that his wife, unlike other politicians' wives, did not own expensive jewelry or clothes.

"I should say this, that Pat doesn't have a mink coat," Nixon stated. "But she does have a respectable Republican cloth coat. And I always tell her that she'd look good in anything. . . . We did get something, a gift after the election. It was a little cocker spaniel dog, black and white spotted.

In 1952 Nixon used the new media of television to persuade millions of Americans that he was not, nor ever had been, involved in financial scandal.

And our little girl Tricia, the six-year-old, named it Checkers. And you know, the kids, like all kids, love the dog and I just want to say this right now, that regardless of what they say about it, we're going to keep him." His address came to be known as the "Checkers" speech because of the attention the little dog Checkers received.

Nixon then told the audience he did not want to do anything to hurt Eisenhower's chances of being elected president. So he volunteered to resign from the ticket if that was what Republicans wanted. Nixon told people to write or send a telegram stating their opinion to the Republican National Committee.

Nixon was not sure how well the speech went, especially because he spoke too long and his time ran out, meaning the broadcast was cut off while he was still talking. But soon it became apparent that Nixon was a hit. Republican leaders all over the country received hundreds of thousands of telegrams urging them to keep Nixon on the ticket. Eisenhower himself called the speech magnificent. He invited Nixon and his wife to visit a few days later, at which time Eisenhower told Nixon that he was sticking with him. At a rally later that day, Eisenhower called Nixon a man of courage and honor.

The speech made Nixon famous. As a result, the Eisenhower-Nixon ticket won in November by a margin of more than seven million votes. It was the first time Republicans had won the presidency in twenty years. The speech, and the subsequent election victory, demonstrated to politicians and journalists how powerful a tool television could be in getting a message directly to voters.

Nixon, by luck and by skill, proved to be a good—even great—vice president. Eisenhower was sixty-two years old when elected. He was often ill, so Ike needed Nixon to be an active vice president, especially in September 1955 when Eisenhower had a heart attack. Nixon ran the country for nearly two months.

Despite Ike's reliance on his vice president, Nixon had to battle to stay on the ticket when Eisenhower decided to run for reelection in 1956. The next vice president would have a clear advantage in succeeding Eisenhower as president, and Ike thought Nixon was still too young for the job.

Nixon had always been controversial, and Eisenhower thought Nixon could be a political liability in 1956.

Nixon created a lot of strong negative feelings in people, and Ike was worried that this dislike of Nixon would affect him and other Republican candidates.

But Nixon convinced Eisenhower that he could help his reelection. He insisted that he was incredibly loyal to the president. Also, Nixon pointed out that he, not Eisenhower, was the one who took on the Democrats and voiced unpopular decisions so that Eisenhower could stay above the battles. Despite his misgivings, Eisenhower kept Nixon as his vice presidential running mate. Again they won an overwhelming victory. This time the Eisenhower-Nixon ticket won by more than nine million votes. The pair won 457 electoral college votes to 74 for the Democrats.

Though not officially tallied, vote counts clearly favored the Eisenhower-Nixon ticket on election night 1956.

The victory alarmed Democrats and other liberals who did not like Nixon, because Eisenhower's poor health meant Nixon could become president at any time. Even if nothing happened to Eisenhower, the fact that Nixon was vice president meant he would be in a very visible job for eight years. Chances were good that Nixon could become the Republican candidate for president in 1960.

In 1957 Eisenhower again suffered health problems, this time a stroke. Nixon was acting president once again. For a time, as Eisenhower hovered near death, it seemed as if Nixon would indeed become president. Even when Eisenhower recovered, his ill health continued. He often sent Nixon to stand in for him abroad.

As vice president, Nixon visited more than sixty countries and traveled about 160,000 miles. He made trips to Asia, Africa, South America, and Europe. On some of these trips, Nixon came home as a hero, after standing up to confrontations.

In 1958, for example, Nixon and his family visited several countries in South America. In Peru angry students yelled at Nixon and threw rocks at him because they did not like Nixon and opposed U.S. policies. Nixon called them cowards and even kicked one demonstrator in the leg. Things got worse when Nixon and his wife reached Venezuela. When the Nixons arrived at the airport in Caracas, the capital, an angry crowd spit on them and threw garbage.

Nixon and his wife were quickly placed in cars for a trip through the city, but again they were confronted by another angry mob. This time the cars were attacked with rocks, pipes, cans, and fists. The car windows cracked as people tried to tip over the automobiles. The Nixons recalled being afraid

Vice President Nixon (standing, front car) sustained injuries while greeting a crowd of U.S. supporters and anti-American protesters in Lima, Peru.

for their lives, thinking that the cars might be overturned and set on fire. A truck finally cleared a path and the Nixons were able to escape to safety. Homemade bombs were later found on the route the Nixons were supposed to have traveled.

At one point, Eisenhower put the U.S. military on alert and sent ships to rescue the Nixons. Luckily they escaped without need for military intervention. When the family returned home, Eisenhower and people around the country hailed the Nixons as heroes.

Nixon thought Communists, trying to embarrass him, the United States, and the governments of the host countries, were behind the demonstrations. The United States at the time was supporting numerous Latin American governments run by generals or dictators as a way to contain Communist expansion. The generals were tough on Communists, but also on their own people, which led to many conflicts in the home countries.

Nixon was seen as representing the force that kept the generals in power, so during his trips he became the focus of the demonstrators' anger. Nixon had been a strong foe of Communism before his trip, but the confrontations in Latin America strengthened those feelings. "It made me almost physically ill to see the fanatical frenzy in the eyes of teenagers—boys and girls who were little older than my twelve-year-old daughter, Tricia," Nixon wrote. "My reaction was a feeling of absolute hatred for the tough Communist agitators who were driving children to this irrational state."

In July 1959, Nixon flew to the Soviet Union, the strongest Communist power in the world at the time, and once again enhanced his reputation as an anti-Communist.

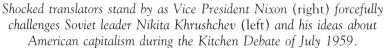

Shocked translators stand by as Vice President Nixon (right) forcefully challenges Soviet leader Nikita Khrushchev (left) and his ideas about American capitalism during the Kitchen Debate of July 1959.

Nixon was in Moscow for the opening of an exhibit on how Americans lived. The visit came at a time when the United States and the Soviet Union were engaged in a political battle to see who could be the most powerful country on earth. Each side believed that its system of government and economics was the best model to follow. Neither country ever lost a chance to tell the world why communism or capitalism was better.

The leader of the Soviet Union, Nikita Khrushchev, was there to greet Nixon. During a tour of a display showing the typical U.S. home, the two men stopped in front of a model kitchen, where they engaged in a spirited debate about whether life was better under communism or capitalism. At one point, Nixon stuck his finger in Khrushchev's chest. Pictures of Nixon standing up to Khrushchev were printed in just about every newspaper in the United States. This confrontation, known as the "Kitchen Debate," once again turned Nixon into an anti-Communist hero because it showed him standing up to the person seen as the leader of the Communists.

Propelled by this increased popularity, Nixon returned to the United States feeling confident. He felt ready for the biggest moment of his life: winning the nomination as the Republican candidate for president in 1960. It seemed likely that Nixon would not only be the Republican candidate, he would also be the heavy favorite to win. The only thing Nixon did not count on was a man named John Fitzgerald Kennedy.

CHAPTER FOUR

NIXON'S FINEST MOMENT

I've got to do it. The time is right.
—Richard Nixon

When Richard Nixon entered the 1960 presidential election, he was probably the second most famous politician in the United States, after President Eisenhower. He had been vice president during one of the most prosperous times in the country's history and had done nothing to embarrass Eisenhower or himself. Polls showed that voters saw him as a strong man who had the experience to deal with the Soviet Union and the rest of the world.

"I was physically, mentally, and emotionally ready for this campaign," Nixon wrote in his memoirs. "I was enthusiastically looking forward to it. I knew it would be an uphill battle, but I felt I could win."

So did a lot of other people—especially because his opponent, Senator John Fitzgerald Kennedy of Massachusetts, was not very well known. Kennedy had been a senator for eight years but was not identified with any particular legislation. He had an image of being more a playboy than a serious politician. Also, Kennedy was a Catholic, and no Catholic had ever been elected president. Many Americans feared that electing a Catholic president would make it possible for the nation to be ruled by the pope, the head of the Catholic Church. To many analysts, the 1960 presidential election looked as if it were going to be a mismatch in Nixon's favor.

In the early part of the race, both men ran strong campaigns. It seemed the only way to judge the two candidates was to have them debate, an old tradition in U.S. politics. But in 1960, for the first time ever, the debates were televised to the entire nation.

Nixon readily agreed to meet Kennedy in a series of four televised debates. Nixon felt especially confident. Not only was he a good debater, he also recalled how well he had done during his televised "Checkers" speech in 1952. As the leading candidate, Nixon could have refused and the debates probably would not have gone on.

The first debate took place on September 26, 1960. In late August, Nixon had injured his knee and was hospitalized for two weeks with an infection. The illness left Nixon weakened and looking pale. The hospital time also set Nixon back in his preparations. It did not help that just as he arrived at the television studio, Nixon banged his injured knee on the car door. It also didn't help that the vice president refused to wear makeup for his television appearance. Without the makeup, Nixon looked pale and older than his forty-seven years to the TV audience. Added to this, Nixon sweated easily, and it was hot in the studio.

Presidential candidates John F. Kennedy and Richard M. Nixon faced off during a series of televised debates in 1960. Nixon often looked stiff and frumpy compared to Kennedy during the debates.

Famous images remain of Nixon looking rumpled and showing a five-o'-clock-shadow beard while Kennedy looked strong and healthy for the 80 million people who watched.

Kennedy had been wearing a dark suit, which looked good on him. Nixon, in contrast, had worn a light brown suit that faded into the tan color of the studio walls. It made Nixon look like a large talking head. A majority of the television audience thought that Kennedy had won the debate, because he looked better than Nixon did. But the debate had also been broadcast on radio, and most of the radio audience thought Nixon had won.

Although Nixon did better in the next few debates, and even wore makeup, he never could recover from the disastrous first debate. Before the debates, Nixon had been ahead in the public opinion polls. After the debates, Kennedy edged slightly ahead of Nixon.

Kennedy also got along well with reporters while Nixon did not. Even Nixon's connection to Eisenhower hurt him.

When asked to name one good thing Nixon had done, Eisenhower told reporters at a news conference that he couldn't think of anything right then. But, he said, give him a week and he'd come up with something.

Even with setbacks, Nixon was able to stay close to Kennedy in the polls. On election day, the first results showed Kennedy winning, then it became almost a tie. Not until the next morning was it declared that Kennedy had won the presidency by about 113,000 votes.

Almost immediately, Republicans began crying foul and claiming that the Democrats had stolen the election. They claimed that illegal votes were cast in Illinois and Texas. Republicans told Nixon that he should challenge the results in court. Many thought he stood an excellent chance of having the vote overturned and being declared president.

George E. Dapples (front, standing) *of the Nixon Recount Committee challenges certification of the presidential vote count in Illinois, alleging tampering.*

Instead of going to court, Nixon made a speech congratulating Kennedy and saying that he would respect the results. Nixon said he had many reasons for doing so. He later wrote, "A presidential recount would require up to half a year, during which time the legitimacy of Kennedy's election would be in question. The effect could be devastating to America's foreign relations. I could not subject the country to such a situation. And what if I demanded a recount and it turned out that despite the vote fraud Kennedy had still won? Charges of 'sore loser' would follow me through history and remove any possibility of a further political career. After considering these and many factors, I made my decision and sent Kennedy a telegram conceding the election."

Although Nixon seemed resigned to the situation, those who knew him said that the 1960 election left him bitter because he thought that dirty tricks had cost him the presidency. He apparently vowed never to be on the short end again. After the election, Nixon found himself unemployed for the first time. He wondered what he would do as he headed into what he considered political oblivion, what he called his Wilderness Period.

Nixon thought that Kennedy would be president for eight years, so he decided to run for governor of California and lost by a large margin. Pat Brown was a popular governor, and Nixon had not even lived full time in California since being elected to Congress in 1946. Above all his heart was not really in the race.

On November 7, 1962, the morning after the election, he surprised a group of reporters at a press conference at the Beverly Hills Hilton, one of the most memorable press conferences of all time. "For sixteen years, ever since the

Nixon announces his withdrawal from politics in 1962, assuring the press they won't have "Nixon to kick around anymore."

Hiss case, you've had a lot of fun—a lot of fun—that you've had an opportunity to attack me and I think I've given as good as I've taken," he told the astonished reporters. "I leave you gentlemen now and you will now write it. You will interpret it. That's your right. But as I leave you, I want you to know—just think how much you're going to be missing. You won't have Nixon to kick around anymore, because gentlemen, this is my last press conference."

Nixon, of course, was wrong. In March 1963, he appeared on television, on the *Jack Paar Show,* a popular talk show. During the program, he announced that he wanted to remain active in public life and was not retiring from politics. After that, Nixon accepted a job in New York with the old, conservative Wall Street law firm of Mudge, Stern, Baldwin, and Todd. He was made a senior partner, and his name was put first, before Mudge, in the firm's name.

Nixon thought that living in New York would help him financially because he would earn a high salary there. Being on the East Coast, he reasoned, also would allow him to stay close to the corridors of power in Washington. In 1963 his book *Six Crises* was published, which put him back in the public spotlight.

In his new job for the law firm, Nixon traveled all over the world to visit clients. But working a steady job soon grew boring, and he considered getting back into politics. When Kennedy was assassinated in Dallas, Texas, on November 22, 1963, many people assumed that Nixon would jump into the 1964 presidential race. But Nixon knew that Vice President Lyndon Johnson would be the sentimental choice of the country because he had become president after Kennedy's death and was seen as carrying on Kennedy's tradition. Nixon decided to stay out of the 1964 race, which Johnson won easily over Republican Barry Goldwater. Republican candidates for the House and Senate also lost several races.

Nixon took advantage of the defeats, however, by making himself useful to Republican candidates who wanted to run in 1966. Nixon was still well known, so he traveled to nearly every state, making speeches on behalf of more than one hundred candidates. In this way, Nixon became a respected national figure again, at least among Republicans. When the Republicans made a comeback in 1966, many of them owed Nixon big favors.

In January 1967, Nixon told advisers that he was going to run for president again. But he decided to keep a low profile so that he would not have to answer a lot of questions from the press and other candidates. Nixon decided to take a series of trips abroad because he wanted to renew contacts with foreign leaders and also get a firsthand look at political situations around the world. He traveled as a private citizen to Western Europe and the Soviet Union in

March, then to Japan, Taiwan, and South Vietnam a month after that. He then traveled to Latin America in May and finished with trips to Africa and the Middle East in June. He met with presidents and generals and gave private speeches to political and business leaders during his travels.

On February 2, 1968, Nixon announced at the Holiday Inn in Manchester, New Hampshire, that he was again running for president of the United States. "I knew that Pat was not in favor of my running, and that was the one factor that finally weighed most heavily in my mind against it,"

Nixon recalled. "But I had increasingly come to understand that politics was not just an alternative occupation for me. It was my life. Although it would be a long, hard road, I felt that this time I could win." Nixon felt ready to come in from the wilderness.

✧ ──────────

Nixon stunned the press on February 2, 1968, when he dramatically announced his return to politics and his bid for the presidency.

CHAPTER FIVE

PRESIDENT NIXON

*That will be the great objective of this administration
at the outset, to bring the American people together.*
—Richard Nixon

In 1968 the United States seemed to be coming apart. The Vietnam War was raging in Southeast Asia, and hundreds of U.S. soldiers were being killed each week. In the United States, hundreds of thousands of people—mostly college students—protested the policies of President Lyndon Johnson, who had greatly escalated U.S. involvement in the war during his term in office. (During the war, U.S. troops fought alongside South Vietnamese troops against the Communist forces of North Vietnam, who were trying to unite the Vietnamese people under Communist rule.) When civil rights leader Martin Luther King Jr. was assassinated on Thursday, April 4, riots broke out in many U.S. cities.

Into this chaos stepped Richard Nixon, who seemed like a politician from another era. Nixon had spent most of the

1960s on the political sidelines, but he promised a new leadership to restore order. Most important, Nixon promised to end the war in Vietnam with a secret plan.

Nixon supported the war as a means to block Communist expansion in Southeast Asia. He wanted to withdraw gradually from Vietnam. His plan was to remove U.S. troops and replace them with South Vietnamese soldiers fighting to defend their homeland. He faced an uphill battle, however, because people wanted to end the war without delay.

Antiwar feeling was so strong that President Lyndon Johnson had decided not to run for reelection. The strongest candidates, in fact, seemed to be antiwar candidates, such as Robert F. Kennedy and Eugene McCarthy. Kennedy, building on his family name and the memory of his dead brother, seemed well on his way to winning the Democratic nomination and probably the presidency. But on June 4, just after winning the California primary election, Robert Kennedy was shot to death by an assassin, throwing the election and the country into chaos.

In August the Republicans ran an incident-free national convention in Miami, Florida. They nominated Nixon for their presidential candidate on August 7, 1968.

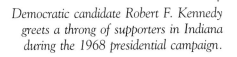

————————— ✧

Democratic candidate Robert F. Kennedy greets a throng of supporters in Indiana during the 1968 presidential campaign.

The following day, Nixon chose Spiro T. Agnew, the governor of Maryland, as his running mate.

Three weeks later, delegates to the 1968 Democratic Convention in Chicago, Illinois, nominated Hubert H. Humphrey for president. The convention was marred by rioting and fighting between police and antiwar demonstrators. "Many were sincere protesters against the Vietnam War," Nixon later wrote, "but some were little more than semiprofessional agitators and educated hoodlums. . . . Like millions of other Americans watching television that night, I did not believe my eyes. . . . Television magnified the agony of Chicago into a national debacle." The convention and the turmoil were televised all over the United States, making it seem as if the Democrats had lost control of their own party. Nixon benefited greatly. Humphrey had been Johnson's vice president, which meant he could not distance himself from the Vietnam policies of the Johnson administration. Humphrey also was not nearly as dynamic as Robert Kennedy had been, so Nixon would not suffer by comparison.

In a brilliant move, Nixon chose Chicago as the place to deliver the central message of his campaign: law and order was what the United States needed to get back to normal. "This is a nation of laws," he told the crowd, "and as Abraham Lincoln has said, 'No one is above the law, no one is below the law,' and we're going to enforce the law and Americans should remember that we're going to have law and order."

Nixon traveled through the city in a large, orderly caravan of cars without violence. Almost half a million people came out to cheer him.

In 1968 Nixon's words drew cheers and votes from the electorate. The people who especially liked the message, and

With the United States in turmoil over the Vietnam War and the assassinations of Martin Luther King Jr. and Robert F. Kennedy, Nixon's "law and order" campaign appealed to a troubled nation.

the ones it was intended for, Nixon liked to call "the silent majority." Nixon called these people the forgotten Americans, who did not get the attention of politicians because they did not organize or shout. It was not long before Nixon was running ahead of Humphrey in the polls.

Humphrey could not seem to cut into Nixon's lead as the campaign dragged on. The one boost Humphrey got was when President Johnson stopped the U.S. bombing in North Vietnam just before the election. It helped Humphrey in the polls, but it was not enough to overcome Nixon.

Nixon, with family, raises his arms in his trademark victory gesture during a celebration of his win over Democratic presidential candidate Hubert H. Humphrey on November 6, 1968.

The election was close. Nixon wasn't declared the winner until the morning after the election. Ironically, Illinois was the state that put him over the top. This time the state Nixon thought had cost him the victory in 1960 helped his political comeback.

As if the election victory wasn't enough, Nixon got even more good news later in the year. On December 22, his youngest daughter, Julie, married David Eisenhower, the grandson of former president Dwight D. Eisenhower. Less than a month later, Richard Milhous Nixon was sworn in as the thirty-seventh president of the United States. His dream had come true.

CHAPTER SIX

A NIGHTMARE CALLED VIETNAM

The greatest honor history can bestow is the title of peacemaker. . . . If we succeed, generations to come will say. . . that we mastered our moment.

—Richard Nixon

Nixon had seen many signs and posters as he traveled the country during the 1968 campaign. The sign he remembered most was held by a teenage boy in Deshler, Ohio. It read, "Bring us together." Nixon decided to make that the theme of his inauguration speech in January 1969.

At the outset of 1969, bringing people together seemed almost impossible. Nixon's margin of victory had not been as large as he would have liked. During his inauguration, thousands of people marched on Washington, D.C., to protest both Nixon's election and the Vietnam War. This meant that in order to bring the country together, he would have to do something spectacular and historic.

THE VIETNAM WAR

The Vietnam War officially lasted from 1957 until 1975. But the seeds of the conflict were planted decades earlier as Vietnam fought to gain its independence from France, which had ruled the area as colonial occupiers since 1884. The Vietnamese finally defeated the French at the battle of Dien Bien Phu in July 1954.

A 1954 treaty to end the war was signed in Geneva, Switzerland. One of the key points of the agreement was the division of the country into North and South Vietnam. Ho Chi Minh became head of North Vietnam under a Communist government. Ngo Dinh Diem became president of South Vietnam under a republican government. The two Vietnams were supposed to hold elections in 1956 to unify the country and decide whether the new nation would be Communist or not. In an effort to prevent Vietnam from becoming a Communist country, the United States supplied South Vietnam with economic, political, and military aid.

Diem refused to go along with the election to unify the country. Instead, in 1957 he asked the United States for more help because the Communists in the north were trying to take over South Vietnam by force. The United States sent civilian and military advisers to help the South Vietnamese battle the Vietcong, as the Communist forces were called. The U.S. personnel were not supposed to fight. They were there only to provide information and advice to Diem's government.

Diem passed many strict laws, which made him unpopular in his country. He turned to undemocratic policies, and many people were arrested simply for being suspected of supporting the Vietcong. While the United States supplied South Vietnam, the Soviet Union and China supplied the Vietcong with military supplies to help them fight the U.S.-backed South Vietnamese army.

On November 1, 1963, Diem's own generals, upset that he had not defeated the rebels, took over the country. Diem was killed the next day. By this time, the number of U.S. advisers in South Vietnam had increased to 16,000. Opinion in the United States was divided between sending more support and withdrawing completely from Vietnam. The situation threatened to draw the United States into a shooting war.

In August 1964, it was reported that North Vietnam attacked a U.S. ship anchored in the Gulf of Tonkin. Lyndon B. Johnson, who was president at the time, asked Congress to give him the power to take "all necessary measures to repel any armed attack against the forces of the United States and to prevent further aggression." On August 7, Congress passed the Tonkin Gulf Resolution, approving these powers. Johnson ordered air attacks against North Vietnam.

In March 1965, Johnson sent the first U.S. combat forces to Vietnam. The U.S. forces rose from 60,000 in 1965 to more than 543,000 in 1969. The United States did not try to conquer North Vietnam. American leaders hoped their superior firepower would force North Vietnam and the Vietcong to stop fighting. North Vietnamese leaders, however, relied on surprise and mobility, and these tactics worked well.

As more American soldiers were killed, the war became extremely unpopular in the United States. When Richard Nixon was elected president in 1968, one of his promises was to pull the United States out of the war.

Nixon (center) *greets U.S. troops in South Vietnam, 1969.*

Nixon thought that a president should be bold in the policies he followed. In order to be remembered as a great president, Nixon believed he would have to create a new world order with the United States at its center. He started out by seeking to portray himself as a peacemaker who would bring an end to the Vietnam War. "The greatest honor history can bestow is the title of peacemaker," Nixon had said during his inaugural address in 1969. "This honor now beckons America. If we succeed, generations to come will say of us now living that we mastered our moment, that we helped make the world safe for mankind. This is our summons to greatness." By the time he took office, the war had claimed the lives of 30,000 U.S. soldiers and more than one million Vietnamese.

Nixon hoped to accomplish his new world order by gathering about him a group of men who would be completely loyal and who would protect him from those he perceived as his enemies. He chose H. R. Haldeman as his chief of staff. He named John Ehrlichman as the person who would be in charge of national, or domestic, issues. Both men were longtime Nixon supporters. Finally, he selected as his national security adviser and top foreign policy aide, a little-known Harvard professor named Henry Kissinger.

Kissinger became the main architect of Nixon's policy to withdraw from Vietnam and bring U.S. soldiers home. Even before the inauguration, in fact, Nixon and Kissinger discussed how to end the war but still not abandon South Vietnam. Nixon ordered Kissinger to meet with a French businessman named Jean Sainteny, who knew the political leaders of North and South Vietnam. Kissinger gave Sainteny notes that were passed to the North Vietnamese leaders saying the United States wanted to start peace talks. It took years, but this initial contact eventually developed into actual negotiations that ended the war.

Henry Kissinger

While preliminary talks with the North Vietnamese were taking place, Nixon decided to pursue the key to his strategy of getting the United States out of the war: replacing U.S. troops with South Vietnamese troops. He called this process the Vietnamization of the war. Nixon hoped to supply and train enough South Vietnamese to take the place of the American troops. In the summer of 1969, Nixon announced that the first U.S. troops, 25,000 in all, were headed home.

Once this war policy was in place, Nixon also launched a visionary policy on new ways to deal with the Communist powers of the world, the Union of Soviet Socialist Republics and the People's Republic of China. In essence, Nixon was trying to move beyond the post-World War II era and end the Cold War.

Nixon realized that the Soviet Union, which had been trying to match the United States in nuclear weapons in what became known as the arms race, had become almost as powerful as the United States. The only way to stop the Soviets from outdistancing the United States was to freeze,

The nation's tolerance for the war in Vietnam was wearing thin by 1969. Protesters marched on Washington, D.C., and throughout the United States.

✧ ──────────────

or even reduce, the stockpiles of nuclear missiles. Nixon sent diplomats, scientists, and arms experts to the Soviet Union to start negotiating an arms limitation treaty. At the same time, Nixon was smart enough to realize that China, with more than one billion people, would soon be one of the great powers of the world.

But Nixon's successes were tempered, and, in fact, threatened, when people who had been waiting for him to bring peace grew tired of waiting. In October 1969, less than a year after Nixon was elected, more than 200,000 protesters marched on Washington to demand an end to the war. The protests soon spread to the rest of the country. Almost overnight Nixon's presidency threatened to go the way of Lyndon Johnson's. Nixon, however, vowed not to give in to the demonstrators. He said that U.S. foreign policy would not be made in the streets of the capital.

The demonstrators were determined that Nixon should listen to what they had to say. "The president of the United

States said nothing you young kids would do would have any effect on him," comedian Dick Gregory said while speaking at one protest. "Well, I suggest to the president of the United States if he want [sic] to know how much effect you youngsters can have on the president, he should make one long-distance phone call to the LBJ [Lyndon B. Johnson] Ranch and ask that boy how much effect you can have."

To counter the protests, Nixon made one of the best speeches of his career. He asked the silent majority for their support. He feared that if the country was divided, recent and ongoing negotiations with the North Vietnamese in Paris, France, might drag on and more U.S. soldiers would die. The speech was a success because more than 80,000 telegrams and letters supporting Nixon's position flooded the White House.

Nixon desperately wanted to end the war. In an effort to do so, he took one of the biggest gambles of his presidency. Instead of reducing the fighting, Nixon escalated it. He ordered the U.S. military to bomb Cambodia, a country neighboring Vietnam on the west.

———————— ✦

Nixon escalated war efforts in Vietnam in 1969 and 1970. Images of growing numbers of fallen U.S. troops in body bags (right) filled the news, troubling the American public.

Although Cambodia was not officially in the war, the North Vietnamese military used Cambodian bases to cross the border into South Vietnam, attack, then retreat into Cambodia. The South Vietnamese and the United States, not wanting to invade a neutral country, stopped at the border.

But in April 1970, Nixon changed all that. He ordered the U.S. military to invade Cambodia and bomb the North Vietnamese bases there. People within his administration warned him not to do so, and three members of the Nixon administration quit in protest. Nixon, however, thought the Cambodian actions were necessary to prove that he and the United States would not be intimidated by war protesters.

Nixon was especially angry with the thousands of anti-war protesters who gathered on U.S. college campuses. He called them "bums" who did not know how lucky they

———————— ✧ ————————

Members of a National Guard unit square off in an effort to control antiwar demonstrators at Kent State University in Ohio on May 4, 1970. The scene turned tragic moments later, with guardsmen opening fire on the students. Four students were killed. Guardsmen were later acquitted of any wrongdoing.

were to be studying on university campuses, while their peers were dying in the hot, steamy jungles of Southeast Asia. The bums remark only angered the protesters more, and it led to some tragic consequences.

On May 4, 1970, National Guard troops fired at student demonstrators after three days of protests at Kent State University in Ohio. Four students were killed, and nine were wounded.

The deaths became the focus of songs and further protests around the country. Demonstrations at hundreds of colleges forced the schools to close. The National Guard and police were called out in more than a dozen states to handle rioting. The protests grew so great that the Secret Service ordered special protection for the president at the White House. The agency had buses brought in to serve as a barricade in front of the White House in case it was attacked.

"It was like living in a bunker in the White House," said Charles Colson, one of Nixon's top aides. "I mean, we'd look out in the streets and see thousands of people protesting. You literally were afraid for your life. There were times that I remember saying, 'I can't believe this is the United States of America, a free country,' and here we are in the White House with barricades up and buses around the White House and tear gas going off and thousands, hundreds of thousands of protesters out in the streets and troops sitting there."

The situation deeply troubled Nixon, who didn't understand why people were so angry about the way he was conducting the war. Shortly after the Kent State killings, Nixon drove to the Lincoln Memorial in Washington, D.C., where thousands of protesters were spending the night.

A pressured President Nixon speaks to a doubtful crowd in Washington, D.C., assuring them of the importance of the war in Vietnam and his commitment to ending the war quickly and successfully.

———————————— ✧ ————————————

He talked to several of them but was met with deep anger and resentment. Aides traveling with him remembered thinking that it was a weird situation—the world's most powerful man standing in a dark business suit trying to understand protesters wearing peace signs, bandanas, and tie-dyed T-shirts.

The pressures on Nixon increased with the protests. In response, Nixon started to believe that people were out to get him, and he grew suspicious of everyone. He started focusing on people he considered his enemies. He even started compiling an enemies list, which included entertainers such as actor Paul Newman, media representatives such as cartoonist Paul Conrad of the *Los Angeles Times,* several Democratic political leaders and fund-raisers, as well as labor leaders and businessmen Nixon thought supported Democrats. Nixon decided to install microphones and a tape recording system in his White House office to document what people were saying and doing.

CHAPTER SEVEN

PLUMBING CHINA

*Let us drink to generations to come who may
have a better chance to live in peace
because of what we have done.*
—Richard Nixon

On June 12, 1971, the president's daughter Tricia married Edward Cox, a Princeton University graduate and a second-year law student at Harvard University. The wedding took place in the White House Rose Garden. No members of the House and Senate were among the four hundred guests. People who saw President Nixon that day say it was one of the happiest days of his life. That happiness was shattered, however, when he picked up the *New York Times* the next day to read about his daughter's wedding.

The event was on the front page. But it was overshadowed by an even bigger story: the disclosure of a secret government study on the history of the Vietnam War that showed the government had lied about the conduct of the war.

President Nixon's personal joy over daughter Tricia's marriage (left) on June 12, 1971, was shattered the next day by former government employee Daniel Ellsberg's (right) disclosure of a secret government study of the Vietnam War.

———————— ✧ ————————

Daniel Ellsberg, a former employee at the Defense Department who had become an opponent of the war, gave the documents to the newspaper. Ellsberg hoped that releasing the information, which came to be known as the *Pentagon Papers* (the Pentagon is the headquarters of the Defense Department), might force the Nixon administration to speed up the end of the war.

The revelation was like a bombshell going off at the White House. Aides remember there was panic. Kissinger was especially upset because he thought leaking such sensitive documents could hurt U.S. foreign policy initiatives. Kissinger was afraid that countries such as the Soviet Union, China, and North Vietnam might be afraid to deal with the United States if it could not even keep its own secret documents secret.

Nixon described the disclosure as the biggest leak of classified documents in American history. He had government lawyers file lawsuits asking the U.S. Supreme Court to prevent newspapers such as the *New York Times* and the *Washington Post* from publishing the *Pentagon Papers* because of the dangerous secrets they might reveal. The Court, however, ruled 6–3 in favor of the newspapers. "We had lost our court battle against the newspaper [the *New York Times*] that published the documents, but I was determined that we would at least win our public case against the man I believed had stolen them, Daniel Ellsberg," Nixon said. "I considered what Ellsberg had done to be despicable and contemptible—he had revealed government foreign policy secrets during wartime."

The *Pentagon Papers* leak increased Nixon's paranoia about the press. His paranoia grew as more and more leaks began to appear in newspapers about administration plans for arms talks with the Russians and other policies. Nixon's aides began compiling a daily list of what journalists and television news programs had reported that day. Each morning Nixon got a summary of what was in the news. He would then scribble notes to aides about what they should say to counter the journalists' stories.

Shortly after the publication of the *Pentagon Papers,* Nixon selected Charles Colson as the person to deal with the leaks. Each morning Colson would also get a summary of the previous night's news. Nixon would have marked the summary with comments on what should be done and to whom. Colson recalled that he started his job each morning feeling as if he were going to war with the press.

Nixon and Colson compiled what they called an enemies list—names of people Nixon wanted to punish and publicly embarrass. Included on the list were reporters, celebrities, politicians, educators, and antiwar people. Those on the list were not allowed to visit the White House. Some were targeted, at Nixon's request, for tax audits by the Internal Revenue Service to see if they were cheating on their income tax. Detectives hired by the White House followed others.

Nixon even created a special group to deal with the supposed enemies. The group, called the plumbers, was supposed to plug up all leaks to the media. One of the first targets of the plumbers was Daniel Ellsberg because of his release of the *Pentagon Papers.* The plumbers figured the best way to get people to stop taking Ellsberg seriously was to present him as a mentally disturbed person. The plumbers broke into the office of Ellsberg's psychiatrist on September 3, 1971, over the Labor Day weekend. The group not only stole files and reports but also broke windows, damaged furniture, and generally trashed the place to make it look as if an addict looking for drugs had broken in.

The burglars found nothing in the files to discredit Ellsberg, and the only thing the break-in accomplished was to tie Nixon and his staff to a crime. Nixon later said, "I do not believe I was told about the break-in at the time . . . but I cannot rule it out. I cannot say that had I been informed of it beforehand, I would have automatically considered it unprecedented, unwarranted, or unthinkable . . . . Today the break-in at Ellsberg's psychiatrist's office seems wrong and excessive. But I do not accept that it was as wrong or excessive as what Daniel Ellsberg did."

The situation with Ellsberg and the *Pentagon Papers* only added to the stress Nixon was feeling during the latter half of 1971. The economy was performing badly too. The inflation rate was increasing along with the unemployment rate. An energy crisis was building, resulting in oil shortages and long lines at gas stations. And each day, more and more dead soldiers were flown home from the jungles of Vietnam.

As a result, Nixon had become incredibly unpopular with voters, and he realized he might not be nominated by his party to run for president in 1972. On January 5, 1972, he formally entered the race and set up a committee to run the campaign. He asked Attorney General John Mitchell to resign so he could take over what was known as the Committee to Re-Elect the President (CREEP). The committee was in charge of raising millions of dollars for Nixon's 1972 campaign. Some of it involved illegal fund-raising in which corporations were asked to donate millions of dollars in exchange for favorable rulings from the Nixon administration. The committee also set up slush funds of unreported cash that was to be used to pay for secret operations.

To bolster his early reelection efforts and to save his image and political career, Richard Nixon did the last thing anyone expected. The ultimate Communist-hater decided to visit the People's Republic of China.

In February 1972, Nixon became the first U.S. president to visit Communist China. After the 1949 Communist revolution in China, the United States had refused to recognize, or accept, the Chinese government. Nixon hoped his trip would make it easier for the two countries to establish formal relations and develop business and culture exchanges. The trip is considered one of Nixon's most significant accomplishments as president.

Nixon hoped his trip to China would also improve U.S. relations with the Soviet Union, a longtime rival of China. He thought establishing a closer relationship with China would make the Soviet Union more agreeable to reaching

Chinese officials show President Nixon the Great Wall of China during his historic visit to the country in 1972.

✧ ————————————

treaties and agreements with the United States. Nixon knew that the Russians did not want to have to fight against an alliance of the United States and China. The move seemed to have worked because the Soviet Union agreed to have Nixon visit Moscow in May 1972. The purpose of the summit, as the meeting between the two superpowers was called, was to reduce nuclear arsenals, something Nixon had been seeking for many months.

Before the summit, Nixon faced one more difficult political decision. In early 1972, just before the summit, the North Vietnamese increased their attacks against South Vietnam. If the United States did not respond, the war would probably be lost, along with South Vietnam. If Nixon responded, however, he threatened the fragile opportunity of the summit because the Soviet Union supported North Vietnam with arms and other material.

Nixon's advisers warned him not to retaliate against North Vietnam and take the chance of angering the Soviet Union. Nixon, however, escalated the war to its highest level in years.

He told his aides that the Soviets would think of him as a weakling if he went to the summit without retaliating. He ordered almost nonstop bombing of Hanoi, the North Vietnamese capital, and ordered that the nearby Haiphong Harbor be blocked with mines. It was a huge gamble because the Soviet supply ships traveled through that harbor. But the gamble paid off. South Vietnam was saved, and the Soviet Union did not cancel the summit.

The summit was one of the highlights of Richard Nixon's presidency. He became the first U.S. president to enter the Kremlin, the Soviet seat of government. He and the Soviet leaders were able to reach agreement on some important topics, including reducing nuclear arms and beginning trade and cultural exchanges. Nixon and the Soviet leader Leonid Brezhnev signed the first Strategic Arms Limitation Treaty, which came to be known as SALT.

The Moscow summit capped off a remarkable six months for Nixon. He had gone from being almost forgotten as a political force to being the world's most important politician. He returned home a hero.

─────────── ✧

An amiable President Nixon (left) and Soviet leader Leonid Brezhnev (right) meet for the historic SALT arms treaty.

CHAPTER EIGHT

DROWNING IN WATERGATE

*First [Nixon] was amazed. Then he sat down
and laughed about it. He said two or three times,
"What in God's name were we doing there?"*

—Bebe Rebozo, referring to Nixon's
reaction to the Watergate break-in

On Saturday, June 17, 1972, television networks reported
on the evening news that a group of five bungling burglars
wearing white surgical gloves and carrying cameras had been
arrested at the Watergate headquarters of the Democratic
National Committee (DNC). The men, four Cubans from
Miami, Florida, and a security consultant for the Committee to Re-Elect the President (CREEP), did not resist
arrest when they were caught by a night watchman at the
Watergate, an apartment, hotel, and office complex in
Washington, D.C. "Nobody knows yet why they were
there," said television reporter Garrick Utley. "But I don't
think that's the last we're going to be hearing of this story."
How right he was. The group apparently had been trying

to plant small microphones, called bugs, inside the DNC's headquarters. It seemed that the burglars wanted to know the Democrats' plans to elect their presidential candidate, Senator George McGovern of South Dakota.

Within a week, every major television network, newspaper, and magazine in the country was chasing after the story. It turned out this was the second time the group had broken into the headquarters. The first time was in the spring, but the bugs planted then had not worked. Journalists around the country scrambled to try and figure out what role—if any—Nixon had played in the latest burglary. Newspaper reporters Bob Woodward and Carl Bernstein of the *Washington Post* probably worked the hardest on the story. Through the use of anonymous informants, they stayed ahead of the competition.

Relying on an unnamed inside source known as "Deep Throat," investigative Washington Post *reporters Bob Woodward* (left) *and Carl Bernstein* (right) *exposed the tangled web of the Watergate scandal to the world.*

WATERGATE

Watergate has become a familiar term for the break-in, cover-up, and scandal that forced Richard Nixon to resign as president on August 9, 1974. At that time, it was the biggest political scandal in U.S. history.

The original term Watergate came from the fact that the break-in that toppled Nixon happened at the Watergate office complex on June 17, 1972. A guard at the Watergate called police to report a probable break-in in progress. Three Washington, D.C., police officers caught five burglars in the act. The men were breaking into the headquarters of the Democratic National Committee headquarters at the office building. The men were wearing rubber gloves and were trying to plant listening devices, or bugs, inside the Democratic headquarters. The police arrested the burglars and took them to the police station.

The men arrested were: James W. McCord, also known as Edward Martin, a former Central Intelligence Agency (CIA) employee and the security director for President Nixon's Committee to Re-Elect the President; Frank Sturgis, also known as Frank Fiorini, a U.S. citizen who also served as an officer in the Cuban military; Eugenio R. Martinez, a Cuban who worked as a real estate agent; Virgilio R. Gonzalez, a locksmith and a Cuban citizen; and Bernard L. Barker, also a native of Cuba who worked part time for the CIA. (The Cubans' connection with the CIA began after Fidel Castro took over in Cuba in 1959. Many Cubans left for the United States because they did not agree with his politics.)

The five men were indicted, or formally charged, on charges of burglary, wire tapping, and conspiracy on September 15, 1972. Two other men, G. Gordon Liddy and E. Howard Hunt, were indicted for the same crime that day because it was discovered that they helped plan the break-in. Hunt had worked for the CIA for twenty-one years and also had worked as a consultant to the Nixon White House. Hunt's name and telephone number were found in address books belonging to the burglars. Liddy, who later became famous as an actor and radio talk show host, was a former FBI agent who, in 1971, had started working for Nixon as a staff assistant. He then joined the Committee to Re-Elect the President as a lawyer in charge of intelligence gathering.

The investigative reporting of *Washington Post* reporters Bob Woodward and Carl Bernstein exposed and unraveled the tangled and twisted case. The *Washington Post,* and its publisher Katharine Graham, won the Pulitzer Prize, the highest award in print journalism, for public service in 1973.

Four of the five Watergate break-in defendants stand with their attorney, Henry Rothblatt (center). The men are (from left to right) Virgilio Gonzalez, Frank Sturgis, Bernard Barker, and Eugenio Martinez.

Nixon had not ordered the break-ins, and no evidence that he did so has ever been produced. In fact, it does not appear that he even knew about the burglaries or what his reelection committee was doing. Nixon recalls that he didn't learn about the June break-in until the next morning, when he read an article in the *Miami Herald* while vacationing in Key Biscayne, Florida. "It sounded preposterous: Cubans in surgical gloves bugging the DNC," said Nixon. "I dismissed it as some sort of prank."

The Watergate break-in marked the beginning of the end of Nixon's presidency. After learning about the break-in, Nixon and his advisers began devising ways to keep people from finding out that the burglars worked for CREEP, Nixon's reelection committee.

Nixon told Haldeman that the break-in should be made to look as if the Cubans were behind it so the White House would not be blamed. Nixon said that Cubans hated McGovern because he was sympathetic to Cuban president Fidel Castro. Castro was a revolutionary who had led a guerrilla war to overthrow Cuban dictator Fulgencio Batista y Zaldívar in 1959. The rebels then set up a Communist government with Castro as its head, and the United States broke off relations with Cuba. McGovern wanted to normalize diplomatic relations with Cuba, which angered Cubans living in the United States.

About a week after the burglars were caught, Nixon suggested that the best way to convince the Cuban burglars to go along with the story was for Nixon's friends to give them money to pay for their legal battle and for living expenses. Nixon told aids the White House had, through donations to CREEP, a secret fund that could be used for such purposes.

In essence the president of the United States was saying that these men should be bribed.

Then Haldeman suggested that the FBI, which was investigating the case, could be thrown off the track by making it seem as if the CIA was behind the break-in. The CIA is a government agency that gathers information about foreign governments and certain nongovernmental groups that engage in terrorism or organized crime. The CIA is the nation's spy agency, sometimes performing covert (secret) operations and break-ins to obtain information. Nixon, who worried that his political opponents would take advantage of the arrests, agreed that it was a good idea to mislead the FBI. Nixon said the FBI should be told that "we just feel that it would be very detrimental to have this thing go any further." The conversation between Nixon and Haldeman was caught on tape, using the recording system Nixon had installed in his office.

Nixon didn't think the investigation would go very far. He focused his attention on the upcoming Republican National Convention in Miami, Florida, where he expected to be overwhelmingly renominated as the Republican presidential candidate. He wanted the victory over the Democrats in November to be historic. He wanted to win by the biggest margin ever in a presidential election.

Nixon set about campaigning not as a Republican, but as "the president." He distanced himself from other Republicans and did not engage in partisan politics during the campaign. Nixon's lack of support for Republican candidates hurt them, and their losses made it impossible for Republicans to take control of the House and Senate.

But Nixon won a historic victory. Even as FBI and Senate investigations into the Watergate break-in were heating up, he defeated his Democratic opponent, George McGovern, by the widest margin of any U.S. presidential election. Nixon received more than 60 percent of the vote, while McGovern got only 37 percent. Nixon, it turned out, won every state but Massachusetts.

After the election, Nixon spent much of his time trying to find a way to finally end the Vietnam War, which was still going on four years after he had promised to end it. The solution that Nixon came up with shocked almost everyone.

In December 1972, Nixon ordered a brutal, around-the-clock bombing attack on Hanoi and Haiphong. The Christmas bombing, as it came to be known, lasted for twelve days. It was the most intense bombing of the entire war. Nixon hoped to scare the North Vietnamese and force them to finally sign a peace treaty with the United States.

Since the June 1972 break-in, however, the White House staff had spent more and more time covering up the Democratic National Committee burglary and the president's connection to it. Secret money from funds controlled by CREEP and by Nixon had been used to pay more than $350,000 in bribes to the burglars to keep them from telling the truth. Nixon's aides lied to grand juries, the FBI, and the public about their role in the affair. John Dean, the president's lawyer, was put in charge of making sure the cover-up stayed in place. As part of his duties, he met almost daily with Nixon to tell him what was happening with the Watergate cover-up and related affairs.

The cover-up began unraveling when Dorothy Hunt, the wife of the break-in organizer Howard Hunt, died in a plane crash in Chicago shortly before the trial began. In Mrs. Hunt's purse was $10,000 in cash that she had been carrying to pay off the burglars. In early January 1973, the trials of the Watergate conspirators began in Washington before U.S. District Judge John J. Sirica.

The Honorable John Sirica

———— ◇ ————

Later that month, just ten days after Nixon had been inaugurated for his second term, G. Gordon Liddy and James W. McCord were convicted of conspiracy for their roles in the Watergate burglary. The two former Nixon aides were two of seven men found guilty in the Watergate case. The five other men who were convicted along with Liddy and McCord had pleaded guilty to conspiracy early in the trial.

Meanwhile, although many people in the United States were condemning Nixon for the Christmas bombing attacks, the bombings did force North Vietnam to accept a deal. Within a month of the bombing, the North Vietnamese returned to Paris for negotiations. Nixon had finally accomplished what he had promised. On January 27, 1973, the United States, North Vietnam, South Vietnam, and the Vietcong (the Communist revolutionary force in South Vietnam) signed a cease-fire agreement.

Only President Nixon, as the political picture at left illustrates, remained seemingly untouched by the Watergate scandal, even after months of hearings and trials.

✧ ——————————

After the Watergate convictions, Nixon asked for the resignation of everyone in his administration so it would look as if he were really starting over. The move stunned even his closest aides. Nixon spent most of the next two months at Camp David, a quiet, rural, presidential residence in Maryland, reviewing old and new appointees.

About the same time, the Senate was organizing a special Watergate Committee to hold hearings to look into the burglary, the cover-up, and the Committee to Re-Elect the President. Howard Hunt then demanded that Nixon's people pay him another $120,000, or he would expose the connection between the burglary, the White House staff, and Nixon himself. In a meeting with Dean, Nixon authorized more bribery money.

In March, within two months after the signing of the cease-fire agreement, thousands of U.S. troops started coming home from South Vietnam. All prisoners of war held by Vietnam were supposed to be released. Nixon's popularity was the highest it had ever been. But Watergate refused to go away.

On March 23, 1973, the cover-up collapsed. James McCord sent a letter to Judge Sirica, who was getting ready to sentence him and the other defendants. In the letter, McCord wrote that he and the others had been acting on orders from the White House. Nixon needed a way to explain to the public what had happened, so he asked John Dean to write a report. Dean hesitated because he thought Nixon was setting him up to take the fall for the burglary and cover-up. Instead of writing the report, Dean started talking to the Senate investigators about what the president knew and when the president knew it.

Dean's defection stunned Nixon, who realized that his lawyer could lead the Senate investigators directly to the president. Nixon called Dean to appeal to his loyalty, noting that he, as president, had given the young lawyer a prominent job. But this did not work. Instead, Nixon's calls made Dean work even more closely with investigators. He told them about the break-in at Daniel Ellsberg's psychiatrist's office.

James McCord (left, with wiretapping equipment) and Nixon attorney John Dean (right) implicated the president in the Watergate scandal in 1973.

The information provided further proof that the Nixon White House was deeply involved in the scandal.

The political pressure on Nixon grew so strong from Congress and the news media that Nixon fired his two top aides, John Ehrlichman and H. R. Haldeman. During an emotional meeting in April, Nixon asked for their resignations. They had become political liabilities to the president. "He began to really cry and I didn't know what to do 'cause I had just never seen him out of control this way," Ehrlichman recalled. "At some point he asked me if there was anything that he could do for me. I said, 'Yeah, I'd like you to explain this all to my kids, because I'm having trouble explaining to them why you would do this.' And he didn't respond to that. So we ended up in a hug. We hugged each other and I could see that he had said everything that he could and that was the end of it."

The pressure intensified as the U.S. Justice Department appointed a special prosecutor, Archibald Cox, to look into the Watergate affair one day after the Watergate hearings began in the Senate chambers on May 17. The hearings were televised nationally, and for months the nation watched in awe as witnesses disclosed the sordid details of the Nixon administration. After several weeks of hearing how Haldeman, Ehrlichman, and others had directed the cover-up, John Dean took the stand to implicate Nixon. Dean testified that Nixon had said he could get a million dollars to pay for the cover-up. At this point, the public knew that Nixon was deeply involved in obstructing justice during the Watergate investigation.

On July 16, 1973, Alexander Butterfield, a former Nixon aide, told the Senate Watergate Committee about the existence of the recording system in the White House and

Judge Charles Fahy (left) *swears in Archibald Cox* (center) *as special Watergate prosecutor as Attorney General Elliot Richardson* (right) *watches.*

the tapes of Nixon's conversations with Dean and others. Nixon was in the hospital at this time, suffering from pneumonia. When Nixon heard what Butterfield had done, he wrote on a notepad that he should have destroyed the tapes.

Nixon's political survival depended on whether he could keep the tapes private. He knew it would involve a legal battle in which he would argue that the tapes were his personal property and not the government's. In this way, Nixon hoped that no one would ever hear what was on them.

When Nixon refused to hand over the tapes to the special prosecutor, the battle went to court. This fight, coming after the John Dean revelations, made it appear that Nixon was attempting to hinder the investigation again. Nixon, seeking to show the public that he had nothing to hide, held a press conference for the first time in more than a year. Nearly all the questions from the press related to Watergate.

President Richard Nixon and wife, Pat (left), *with newly selected Vice President Gerald Ford and his wife, Betty* (right)

———————————— ✧ ————————————

The situation in the White House worsened. On October 10, 1973, Vice President Spiro Agnew was forced to resign. Agnew pleaded no contest to charges of tax evasion after being investigated for taking bribes for building contracts while he was governor of Maryland. Nixon selected Congressman Gerald Ford of Michigan to be the new vice president.

On the same day that Ford was introduced as the new vice president, the Supreme Court ruled that Nixon must turn over his tapes to Archibald Cox and his team of prosecutors. Nixon refused. When Cox continued to insist that Nixon turn over the tapes, Nixon told Attorney General Elliot Richardson to fire Cox from the investigation. Richardson refused to do so because he had promised the public that the Cox investigation would be independent and not subject to political pressure. This so angered Nixon that what followed came to be known as the Saturday Night Massacre. In a matter of hours, Nixon fired Cox. Then Richardson resigned. Nixon then fired Richardson's assistant, who also refused the order to fire Cox. Finally, Nixon ordered the FBI to seal off the offices of Cox and the attorney general.

"The country tonight is in the midst of what may be the most serious Constitutional crisis in its history," newscaster John Chancellor said when he opened his evening news show on NBC that night. "All of this adds up to a totally unprecedented situation, a grave and profound crisis in which the president has set himself against his own attorney general and the Department of Justice. Nothing like this has ever happened before. More than 50,000 telegrams poured in on Capitol Hill [Congress] today, so many Western Union was swamped. Most of them demanded impeaching Mr. Nixon." After the Saturday Night Massacre, more than twenty resolutions were introduced in Congress demanding that Nixon be impeached. (Impeachment is the legal process outlined in the Constitution by which a president is put on trial in Congress and forced out of office if convicted.) Finally Nixon appointed a new special prosecutor, Leon Jaworski, and agreed to turn over the tapes.

Nixon also held another press conference to explain why two tapes were missing and why one had a mysterious eighteen-minute gap. Nixon's secretary, Rosemary Woods, claimed she had accidentally erased the tape while transcribing it. Soon people began to question just how trustworthy Nixon was, how he got his vacation homes, whether he took bribes, whether he

Special Prosecutor Leon Jaworski

had cheated on his taxes. "I made my mistakes, but in all of my years of public life, I have never profited from public service—I have earned every cent," Nixon said at a press conference. "And in all of my years of public life, I have never obstructed justice. And I think, too, that I can say that in my years of public life, that I welcome this kind of examination, because people have got to know whether or not their president is a crook. Well, I am not a crook." These proved to be famous last words for Nixon as his presidency disintegrated. Many of his top aides were indicted by the Watergate Committee.

When the prosecutors demanded the remaining tapes, Nixon faced another court fight that went to the Supreme Court. Instead of releasing the additional tapes, Nixon decided to release twelve hundred pages of transcripts containing typed

pages of all the conversations. The transcripts were edited, but Nixon assured everyone that he was presenting a true picture, warts and all, of what had happened in his White House.

✧ ———————

President Nixon with transcripts of his Oval Office tapes. The Supreme Court ordered him to turn over the tapes to the Justice Department.

Nixon thought this would be enough to convince people that he was complying with the Supreme Court and was not covering up Watergate evidence.

Instead, when people read the transcripts they were disgusted. The transcripts contained swearing and information about illegal wiretaps and other situations that people found unethical. They showed a man who was desperately trying to hang on to power as his world disintegrated around him, according to Henry Kissinger. "The President lived in the stunned lethargy of a man whose nightmares had come true," Kissinger recalled. "Like a figure in Greek tragedy, he was fulfilling his own nature and destroying himself."

On July 27, 1974, as President Richard Milhous Nixon was getting dressed after swimming at a California beach, the House Judiciary Committee in Washington charged him with three articles of impeachment. The committee accused Nixon of obstruction of justice, abuse of power, and contempt of Congress. He faced an impeachment trial in the U.S. Senate, which he was doomed to lose because of the information on the secret tape recordings.

Then the Supreme Court forced Nixon to release what came to be known as the smoking gun, a tape of a conversation Nixon had had with Haldeman on June 23, 1972, that provided direct evidence of criminal guilt. On the tape, the president said the FBI should be deceived and that he (Nixon) did not want the Watergate investigation to go forward. On August 8, 1974, as outrage over the tape increased, Nixon decided he would have to resign because what he had said on the tape was considered obstruction of justice. He scheduled a televised speech to the nation to explain his decision. It was the first time a U.S. president had resigned from office.

"I have never been a quitter," Nixon said. "To continue to fight through the months ahead for my personal vindication would almost totally absorb the time and attention of both the President and the Congress in a period when our entire focus should be on the great issues of peace abroad and prosperity without inflation at home. Therefore, I shall resign the presidency, effective at noon tomorrow. Vice President Ford will be sworn in as president at that hour in this office."

The following day, August 9, 1974, Nixon and his family said good-bye to the White House staff. In an awkward and at times disjointed farewell address, Nixon fought back tears as he evoked the memory of President Theodore Roosevelt. Nixon reminded those around him that greatness came when things were at their worst. "Always give your best," Nixon said before he climbed aboard a helicopter for a ride to the airport and a flight home to San Clemente, California. "Never get discouraged; never be petty; always remember, others may hate you, but those who hate you don't win unless you hate them, and then you destroy yourself."

CHAPTER NINE

THE ULTIMATE COMEBACK

I brought myself down. I gave them a sword.
And they stuck it in. . . . And, I guess, if I'd been
in their position, I'd have done the same thing.
—Richard Nixon

Almost everyone assumed that Nixon's political life was over. Not only was Nixon thought of as one of the most contemptible men in the country, he also faced several lawsuits and the prospect of going to jail for his crimes. "The pounding in the newspapers and on television continued," Nixon recalled. "I was the favorite butt of jokes on the talk shows. Hundreds of [newspaper] columns attacked me. A number of anti-Nixon books were published. Those by critics I understood. Those by friends I found a bit hard to take."

On September 8, 1974, President Gerald Ford surprised many people when he granted Nixon a full pardon for his role in the Watergate affair. Nixon had avoided any penalty, despite the fact that more than seventy of his aides and supporters were convicted and punished for their participation in Watergate. For his part, Nixon issued only a simple statement to the news media regarding the pardon, Watergate, and the impact that it had on the country. "I was wrong in not acting more decisively and more forthrightly in dealing with Watergate, particularly when it reached the stage of judicial proceedings and grew from a political scandal into a national tragedy," Nixon said. "No words can describe the depths of my regret and pain at the anguish my mistakes over Watergate have caused the nation and the Presidency—a nation I so deeply love and an institution I so greatly respect."

Even with the pardon, the post-Watergate period was not easy. Nixon was in bad shape physically and financially.

President Gerald Ford pardons Richard Nixon for his role in the Watergate scandal. Many Americans were outraged by the pardon.

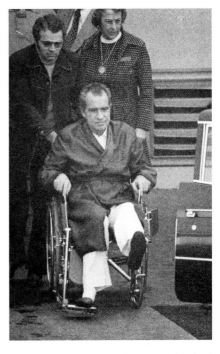

Nixon is wheeled to a waiting limousine to take him home after more than a month in the hospital in 1974.

——————— ✧

Defending himself against various lawsuits had left him with no money. About a week after the pardon, Nixon was hospitalized with a near-fatal illness. Blood clots were discovered in his leg, and for two days it appeared that he would die.

Nixon left the hospital after five weeks, then secluded himself at San Clemente as he tried to recover. Nixon did not speak to the media or in public. For a while, it seemed as if he had disappeared. "There was no precedent for what faced me in the 1970s," Nixon wrote years later. "No one had ever been so high and fallen so low. No one before had ever resigned the presidency."

The only good things that came out of these years, Nixon later recalled, was that he was able to write his memoirs. "With the wounds of body and spirit healed, I was now prepared to deal with my greatest challenge— mental recovery," Nixon wrote. "This was the decisive factor in my decision to write my memoirs . . . it provided the therapy that was needed for a full spiritual recovery by enabling me to put Watergate behind me." Nixon's book, entitled *RN: The Memoirs of Richard Nixon,* was published in 1978. The book focused on Nixon's political life, but much of the book dealt with the former president clarifying his position on Watergate and other controversies.

After he completed his memoirs, Nixon recalls that he faced what he called a life and death decision on his sixty-fifth birthday. He had to figure out what to do with the rest of his life. He knew he could not run for public office again. But he wanted to stay involved in world issues. He decided to travel the world, make speeches, and write books about his opinions.

At about the same time, Nixon agreed to sit down for a series of four televised interviews with journalist David Frost.

The interviews earned Nixon $540,000, but he said all the money went to his lawyers, who had run up huge bills defending him in lawsuits. The biggest controversy arising from the interviews centered on the fact that Nixon

✧ ————————

A series of interviews with respected journalist David Frost (left) revealed little of Nixon's involvement in Watergate.

Nixon continued in public life, giving interviews, attending political functions, and delivering speeches such as this one at Oxford University in England in 1978.

conceded that he had made mistakes during Watergate but refused to apologize or admit that he had abused his power while in office.

In January 1978, Nixon traveled to Washington to attend a memorial service for Hubert H. Humphrey, whom Nixon had defeated in 1968. It was the first time Nixon had returned to the nation's capital since resigning. On November 30, 1978, Nixon gave a speech to a group of students at Oxford University in England. Outside the hall, Nixon was once again greeted by hundreds of protesters, most of them American students studying in England. Some pounded on the doors of Nixon's car; others jumped on the car itself. The yelling could still be heard when Nixon was about to start his speech. The crowd inside the hall, however, was respectful toward Nixon. He recalls getting a standing ovation when he entered to begin his speech. Nixon started his remarks by telling the audience that the demonstrators made him feel at home.

Buoyed by the good reception of the Oxford audience, his first speech to a university group since resigning, Nixon agreed to give a speech in the United States. He spoke to a group of military veterans, members of the American Legion organization, in Mississippi, declaring that he was coming out of exile and returning to public life. He also participated in a question and answer program in France. In January 1979, President Jimmy Carter invited Nixon to the White House as part of a special dinner he was having to celebrate the establishment of normal relations with China. Until this time, the United States had refused to recognize the Communists as the official leaders of China. The process Nixon had begun with China almost seven years before had been completed.

Nixon then began working on a book called *The Real War.* It dealt with world politics and the U.S. role in the world, which he described as focusing on relations between China, the United States, the Soviet Union, Europe, and Japan. The book was a worldwide best seller, which helped Nixon financially and emotionally. "When I completed the book in January 1980, I knew the time had come to leave San Clemente and to return to the arenas in which I could more effectively serve the causes in which I had committed my life," Nixon wrote.

The former president moved to New York City that year to pursue his career as an author more actively. He and Pat then bought an estate in Park Ridge, New Jersey, in 1981, where Nixon continued to write. He published another book, *Leaders,* in 1982, and *Real Peace: A Strategy for the West,* in 1983. This was followed by *No More Vietnams* in 1985.

Energized by the success of his books, Nixon started traveling more than ever as a private citizen, often visiting countries that he had visited as president or vice president. He was received by heads of state all over the world, including China, the Soviet Union, Japan, England, France, Egypt, Saudi Arabia, Bulgaria, Romania, Pakistan, South Korea, Thailand, and Czechoslovakia.

Journalists began speculating that Nixon was preparing for a comeback. They were right to a certain extent. Nixon was coming back into the arena, as he liked to say, but he was doing so as a behind-the-scenes elder statesman who wrote about and discussed policy without running for elective office. During the last part of Nixon's life, almost every president quietly sent Nixon on missions abroad.

To better improve his public image and to try to assure that he would be written about favorably after his death, Nixon began courting the news media. He started to invite selective groups of journalists to his home in New Jersey. After being served dinner, the journalists listened to Nixon talk about world and national affairs. They were then allowed to ask questions.

The move to the East Coast allowed Nixon to be closer to Washington, D.C., and to the newly elected president, Ronald Reagan. Reagan was a fellow Republican, and he often called upon Nixon behind the scenes. Although Nixon was not allowed to speak at the 1984 Republican Convention, Reagan's links to Nixon helped the former president. President George H. W. Bush, who succeeded Reagan, was also a Republican, and he also was an admirer of Nixon. He, too, called upon the former president for advice, again in private.

ˌ In 1986, when Nixon gave a speech to a group of publishers, he received a standing ovation. He was even pictured shaking hands with *Washington Post* publisher Katharine Graham, whose newspaper had been largely responsible for exposing Nixon's Watergate ties. Shortly thereafter, *Newsweek* magazine ran a story and put Nixon's photo on the cover. A big headline said simply, "HE'S BACK: THE REHABILITATION OF RICHARD NIXON."

In 1990 the Richard Nixon Library and Birthplace was built in Yorba Linda, where Nixon had been born. It serves as a storage facility for documents from Nixon's political career and a museum to portray his life. Among the artifacts displayed on the grounds is the home that Nixon's father built. The restoration took place in 1993, the same

(From left to right) *Pat and Richard Nixon with Nancy and Ronald Reagan, George H. W. and Barbara Bush, and Betty and Gerald Ford at the dedication of the Nixon Library and Birthplace in 1990*

Though many did not agree with or condone President Nixon's political tactics, they admired his fighting spirit. His funeral in 1994 was well attended by many dignitaries, including every living U.S. president.

———————————— ✧ ————————————

year that Pat Nixon died. On April 19, 1994, Nixon suffered a stroke and was hospitalized. He died on April 22.

Richard Nixon's death was news all over the world. His photo appeared again after his death on the cover of *Time* magazine. It was the sixty-fifth time that Nixon had been on the cover of the famous magazine, setting a record. Nixon had ordered that he be buried next to his wife near the farmhouse where he had been born. By strange coincidence, the plane that brought Nixon's body home was the same one that the former president had used to fly to California in 1974 when he resigned after Watergate.

"By sheer endurance he was the most important figure of the post-War era," *Time* magazine wrote about Nixon upon his death. The magazine article echoed a sentiment felt by many people across the country.

As a final show of respect, President Bill Clinton declared a national day of mourning in Nixon's honor. He ordered Congress, the New York Stock Exchange, the Supreme Court, and other government services to close. The flags at all government buildings were ordered flown at half-staff. Thousands of people stood in the rain to pay their last respects and watch the funeral procession when Nixon's body arrived in California.

More than 42,000 people later stood in line at the Nixon Library, where Nixon's body lay in state. At one point, the line was reportedly more than three miles long as people waited patiently to pay their final respects. All four living U.S. presidents attended Nixon's funeral.

"Strong, brave, unafraid of controversy, unyielding in his convictions, living every day of his life to the hilt, the largest figure of our time, whose influence will be timeless— that was Richard Nixon," said Bob Dole, a former U.S. senator from Kansas and a close friend of Nixon.

Dole's eulogy continued: "I believe the second half of the twentieth century will be known as the age of Nixon. Why was he the most durable public figure of our time? Not because he gave the most eloquent speeches, but because he provided the most effective leadership. Not because he won every battle, but because he always embodied the deepest feelings of the people he led . . . the man who was born in a house his father built would go on to become this century's greatest architect of peace."

CONCLUSION

In that worse time after Watergate I never gave up. I was always sure that the pendulum would swing.

—Richard Nixon

Senator Dole recalled the last time he had seen Nixon. Dole attended a luncheon in Washington, honoring the twenty-fifth anniversary of Nixon's first inauguration in 1968. As he often did, Nixon spoke without notes and delivered what Dole described as a compelling speech about his vision of America's future.

When Nixon finished, both Democrats and Republicans surrounded him, everyone wanting just one more word with him, one more question about world affairs. After the speech, the eighty-year-old Nixon was supposed to rest in Dole's office, but the office was filled with young workers wanting to get an autograph or simply convey their regards to Nixon. His popularity that day was an indication of just how far he had succeeded in rebuilding his image after the Watergate scandal.

The fascination with Nixon, however, did not end with his death. Journalists, movie producers, writers, and even comedians began taking a new look at Richard Nixon. Since 1994 numerous books, magazines, and newspapers have printed thousands of words about how important he was in the country's history. Some views of Nixon were not flattering. In his book *The Arrogance of Power: The Secret World of Richard Nixon,* British writer Anthony Summers made Nixon out to be someone who drank too much, took too many prescription drugs, and was abusive to family and friends.

Director Oliver Stone's controversial movie *Nixon* made it appear as if Nixon, apart from Watergate, had also been involved in a vast government conspiracy involving wrongdoing during the Vietnam War and the Bay of Pigs invasion of Cuba. (The invasion had been carried out during the Kennedy administration, but planning for it had begun during the Eisenhower administration. Nixon, as Eisenhower's vice president, was aware that it was going to take place.) The Stone movie was widely discredited by critics and historians as being speculative and lacking solid documentation. Over the years, Nixon also was featured as a character in at least six movies or television shows. One movie called *Dick,* which was released in 1999, was a comedy in which Nixon was made to appear as a funny, good-humored guy who was misunderstood.

"If Nixon left office a president repudiated by most Americans, he was also a president of major achievements who in many ways shaped the America of today," *U.S. News & World Report* magazine wrote in a 1999 cover story on Nixon. "Nixon's legacy runs far beyond the political reforms spawned by Watergate. To an extent few people

Despite Watergate, President Nixon had a political career marked by many honorable achievements.

✧ ————————

appreciate, we still live in Richard Nixon's America."

Despite mixed opinion about Nixon, on Saturday, June 30, 2001, a Fullerton, California, woman became the two millionth person to visit the Richard Nixon Library and Birthplace. In the years since Nixon died, it seems he finally achieved the respectability and admiration that he sought while he was alive.

TIMELINE

1913   Nixon is born on January 9 in Yorba Linda, California.

1922   The Nixon family moves to Whittier, California, where Francis Nixon starts a gasoline station.

1925   Nixon's youngest brother, Arthur, dies.

1930   Nixon enters Whittier College.

1934   Nixon graduates from Whittier College; enters Duke University Law School in Durham, North Carolina.

1937   Nixon graduates from Duke University and begins law practice in Whittier.

1940   Nixon marries Patricia Ryan, an aspiring actress and high school teacher.

1942   Nixon enlists in the U.S. Navy during World War II.

1946   Tricia Nixon is born on February 21. Nixon wins his first election, for the U.S. House of Representatives.

1948   Nixon's second daughter, Julie, is born on July 5. Nixon wins reelection to the House of Representatives.

1952   Nixon is elected vice president on the Eisenhower ticket.

1956   Eisenhower and Nixon are reelected.

1958   Nixon and his family tour South America on behalf of the Eisenhower administration.

1959   Nixon visits the Soviet Union.

1960   Nixon makes his first run for the presidency. John F. Kennedy defeats Nixon by a narrow margin.

1962   Nixon loses his bid for governor of California and announces his withdrawal from politics.

1963 The Nixon family moves to New York, where Nixon becomes a partner in a law firm. His first book, *Six Crises,* is published.

1967 Nixon decides to return to politics and make a run for the presidency.

1968 Nixon is elected the thirty-seventh president of the United States; Julie Nixon marries David Eisenhower on December 22.

1969 Nixon is inaugurated president on January 20.

1970 Nixon escalates U.S. involvement the Vietnam War to include bombing and ground raids of Vietcong bases in Cambodia.

1971 Tricia Nixon marries Edward Cox at the White House on June 12. The *Pentagon Papers* are published. Nixon orders the installation of a voice recording system in the Oval Office.

1972 Nixon visits China and the Soviet Union. Burglars working for the Republican National Committee break into the Watergate complex. Nixon is reelected president.

1973 The Vietnam War truce is signed. The Watergate burglars are convicted. The impeachment process against Nixon begins.

1974 Nixon is charged with three articles of impeachment. Nixon resigns the presidency on August 9. Vice President Gerald Ford becomes president. He pardons Nixon on September 8.

1978 Nixon's memoirs are published. He begins traveling the world.

1980 Nixon and wife, Pat, move to the East Coast.

1990 The Richard Nixon Library and Birthplace opens in Yorba Linda, California.

1993 Pat Nixon dies on June 22.

1994 Nixon dies on April 22 in New York. His body is flown to California for burial at the Nixon Library and Birthplace.

Source Notes

8 Martin Weil and Eleanor Randolph, *Washington Post,* April 23, 1994: A01, <http://www.washington post.com/wpsrv/national/longterm/watergate/stories/nixobit.htm> (March 23, 2002).

12–13 Anthony Summers, *The Arrogance of Power: The Secret World of Richard Nixon* (New York: Viking Publishers, 2000), 7.

15 Michael A. Schuman, *Richard M. Nixon* (Springfield, NJ: Enslow Publishers, 1998), 15.

18 Summers, 1.

19 Schuman, 18.

19 Roger Barr, *The Importance of Richard M. Nixon* (San Diego: Lucent Books, 1992), 12.

23 Richard Nixon, *RN: The Memoirs of Richard Nixon* (New York: Grosset & Dunlap, 1978), 29.

24 The American Experience, *The Presidents,* "Nixon," PBS Television, transcript, 1997, <http://www.pbs.org/wgbh/amex/presidents/nf/resource/nixon/nixscript.htm> (May 29, 2001).

26 Schuman, 40.

27 Nixon, *RN: The Memoirs,* 41.

30 Dee Lillegard, *Richard Nixon, The Thirty-Seventh President of the United States* (Chicago: Children's Press, 1988), 45.

34 Richard Nixon, *In the Arena: A Memoir of Victory, Defeat and Renewal* (New York: Simon and Schuster, 1990), 175.

36 Richard Nixon, text of Nixon's "Checkers" speech, <http://www.pbs.org/wgbh/ amex/presidents/ nf/resource/ nixon/primdocs/ checkers.html> (August 17, 2001).

36–37 Ibid.

42 Schuman, 59.

44 Nixon, *RN: The Memoirs,* 214.

48 Ibid.

48–49 Barr, 59.

51 Nixon, *RN: The Memoirs,* 294.

54 Ibid., 317.

54 The American Experience, *The Presidents,* "Nixon," 1997.

60 Ibid.

62–63 Ibid.

65 Ibid.

69 Nixon, *RN: The Memoirs,* 511.

70 Ibid., 514.

74 The American Experience, *The Presidents,* "Nixon," 1997.

78 Nixon, *RN: The Memoirs,* 626.

79 Stanley I. Kutler, *Abuse of Power: The New Nixon Tapes* (New York: The Free Press, 1997), 68.

84 The American Experience, *The Presidents,* "Nixon," 1997.

87 Ibid.

88 Nixon, *RN: The Memoirs,* 957.

89 Summers, 452.

90 Barr, 91.

90 Schuman, 93.

91 Ibid.

92 Barr, 95.

93 Nixon, *In the Arena,* 30.

93–94 Ibid., 33.

96 Ibid., 45.

98 Schuman, 98.

100 Christopher Matthews, *Kennedy and Nixon, the Rivalry That Shaped Postwar America* (New York: Simon and Schuster, 1996), 345.

100 TIME/CNN website, <http://europe.cnn.com/allpolitics/1997/gen/resources/watergate/dole.speech.html> (August 17, 2001).

102–103 Michael Barone, "Nixon's America," *U.S. News & World Report,* September 9, 1999: 1 (cover), US News Online, <http://www.usnews.com> (May 31, 2001).

BIBLIOGRAPHY

The American Experience. *The Presidents.* "Nixon." PBS Television, program transcript, 1997, <http://www.pbs.org/wgbh/amex/presidents/nf/resource/nixon/nixscript.html> (May 29, 2001).

Barr, Roger. *The Importance of Richard M. Nixon.* San Diego: Lucent Books, 1992.

Kutler, Stanley I. *Abuse of Power: The New Nixon Tapes.* New York: The Free Press, 1997.

Lillegard, Dee. *Richard Nixon, The Thirty-Seventh President of the United States.* Chicago: Children's Press, 1988.

Matthews, Christopher. *Kennedy and Nixon, the Rivalry That Shaped Postwar America.* New York: Simon and Schuster, 1996.

Nixon, Richard. *In the Arena: A Memoir of Victory, Defeat and Renewal.* New York: Simon and Schuster, 1990.

————. *RN: The Memoirs of Richard Nixon.* New York: Grosset & Dunlap, 1978.

Schuman, Michael A. *Richard M. Nixon.* Springfield, NJ: Enslow Publishers, 1998.

Summers, Anthony. *The Arrogance of Power: The Secret World of Richard Nixon.* New York: Viking Publishers, 2000.

FURTHER READING AND WEBSITES

Blue, Rose, and Corinne J. Naden, *The Modern Years, 1969 to 2001.* Austin, TX: Raintree Steck-Vaughn, 1998.

Darby, Jean. *Dwight D. Eisenhower.* Minneapolis: Lerner Publications Company, 1989.

Dudley, William, ed. *The Vietnam War: Opposing Viewpoints.* San Diego: Greenhaven Press, 1998.

Fremon, David K. *The Watergate Scandal in American History.* Springfield, NJ: Enslow Publishers, 1998.

Gaines, Ann. *Richard M. Nixon: Our Thirty-Seventh President.* Chanhassen, MN: Child's World, 2001.

Galt, Margot Fortunato. *Stop This War! American Protest of the Conflict in Vietnam.* Minneapolis: Lerner Publications Company, 2000.

Hargrove, Jim. *Richard M. Nixon: The Thirty-Seventh President.* Chicago: Children's Press, 1985.

Herda, D. J. *United States v. Nixon: Watergate and the President.* Springfield, NJ: Enslow Publishers, 1996.

Levy, Debbie. *Lyndon B. Johnson.* Minneapolis: Lerner Publications Company, 2003.

Nixon White House Tapes. <http://www.c-span.org/executive/presidential/nixon.asp>. Users can listen to some of President Nixon's White House tapes at this site presented by the political news network C-SPAN.

Pious, Richard M. *Richard Nixon: A Political Life.* Englewood Cliffs, NJ: Julian Messner, 1991.

Randolph, Sallie G. *Richard M. Nixon, President.* New York: Walker, 1989.

Richard Nixon Library & Birthplace. <http://www.nixonfoundation.org/index.shtml>. The official website for the Nixon Library and Birthplace, offering biographies of Richard M. and Pat Nixon, a Nixon forum, and a virtual research center and tour of the facility.

Ripley, C. Peter. *Richard Nixon.* New York: Chelsea House, 1987.

INDEX

ABOUT THE AUTHOR

Herón Márquez, born in Mexico, moved to California at the age of six. After a short career playing semiprofessional baseball, he took up writing. He has worked as a journalist for such papers as the *Albuquerque Journal, New York Daily News, Los Angeles Times, Santa Barbara News Press,* and the Minneapolis *Star Tribune.* Other titles that Márquez has written for Lerner Publications Company include *George W. Bush* and *Latin Sensations.* Márquez lives in St. Paul, Minnesota, with his wife Traecy.

PHOTO ACKNOWLEDGMENTS

The images in this book are used with the permission of: National Archives, pp. 2, 6, 55, 59, 63 [NWDNS-111-SC-635974], 66 [NLNP-WHPO-MPF-4808-09]; © Bettmann/ CORBIS, pp. 8, 9, 17, 20 (left), 29, 30, 31, 37, 39, 41, 47, 49, 51, 56, 64, 68 (left and right), 75, 83 (left and right), 85, 87, 92, 93, 94, 95; Library of Congress, pp. 10 [31-2501], 16, 82 [LC-USZ62-093125]; Richard Nixon Library & Birthplace, pp. 13, 14, 15, 20 (right), 24; © David J. & Janice L. Frent Collection/CORBIS, pp. 25, 32, 35; © CORBIS, p. 42; Southdale-Hennepin Area Library, p. 46; © Wally McNamee/CORBIS, pp. 53, 62, 73, 77, 88, 98; Independent Picture Service, p. 61; The White House, pp. 72, 103; Chase Ltd., p. 81; Gerald R. Ford Library, p. 86; © Reuters NewMedia Inc./ CORBIS, p. 99.

Cover photo: National Archives